MATHEMATICS FOR PRIMARY AND EARLY YEARS

Developing Subject Knowledge

Second Edition

D0231665

Ways of knowing: language, mathematics and science in early years

This book forms part of The Open University course *Ways of knowing: language, mathematics and science in early years* (E230). This is a 30 point course at level 2 and is part of the Foundation Degree in Early Years.

Details of this and other Open University courses can be obtained from the Student Registration and Enquiry Service, The Open University, PO Box 197, Milton Keynes MK7 6BJ, United Kingdom: tel. +44 (0)845 300 60 90, email general-enquiries@open.ac.uk.

Alternatively, you may visit The Open University website at http://www.open.ac.uk where you can learn more about the wide range of courses and packs offered at all levels by The Open University.

MATHEMATICS FOR PRIMARY AND EARLY YEARS

Developing Subject Knowledge

Second Edition

Heather Cooke

SAGE Publications

Los Angeles · London · New Delhi · Singapore

The Open University
Walton Hall
Milton Keynes
MK7 6AA
United Kingdom
www. open. ac uk

© 2000 and 2007 The Open University

First published 2000
Second edition 2007

Apart from any fair dealing for the purposes of research or private study, or criticism or review, as permitted under the Copyright, Designs and Patents Act, 1988, this publication may be reproduced, stored or transmitted in an form, or by any means, only with the prior permission in writing of the publishers, or in the case of reprographic reproduction, in accordance with the terms of licences issued by the Copyright Licensing Agency. Enquiries concerning reproduction outside those terms should be sent to the publishers.

SAGE Publications Ltd
1 Oliver's Yard
55 City Road
London EC1Y 1SP

SAGE Publications Inc
2455 Teller Road
Thousand Oaks, California 91320

SAGE Publications India Pvt Ltd
B1/I1 Mohan Cooperative Industrial Area
Mathura Road, New Delhi 110 044
India

SAGE Publications Asia-Pacific Pte Ltd
33 Pekin Street #02-01
Far East Square
Singapore 048763

KENT LIBRARIES AND ARCHIVES	
C153275631	
HJ	21/11/2007
510.24372	£19.99

Library of Congress Control Number: 2006940629

British Library Cataloguing in Publication data

A catalogue record for this book is available from the British Library

ISBN 978-1-4129-4609-4
ISBN 978-1-4129-4610-0 (pbk)

Typeset by Pantek Arts Ltd, Maidstone, Kent
Printed and bound in Great Britain by the Cromwell Press, Trowbridge, Wiltshire
Printed on paper from sustainable resources

Contents

Preface

Mathematics for Primary and Early Years: Developing Subject Knowledge is written specifically for people who need to develop their mathematics subject knowledge and understanding.

The task-driven text emphasises strategies and processes and is very different from the usual style of mathematics textbooks. It is written with the needs of the under-confident in mind, with a strong emphasis on active learning. Common mathematical misconceptions are explored. The book includes a self-assessment section and guidance on how to target study effectively.

Companion books in this series are:

English for Primary and Early Years: Developing Subject Knowledge by Ian Eyres.

Science for Primary and Early Years: Developing Subject Knowledge by Jane Devereux.

Acknowledgements

The Mathematics Team

First and Second Edition contributors

Barbara Allen

Heather Cooke

Hilary Evens

Jenny Houssart

Alan Graham

Sue Johnston-Wilder

Eric Love

John Mason

Christine Shiu

First Edition production

Gaynor Arrowsmith, Course Manager

Sue Dobson, Graphic Artist

Sue Glover, Publishing Editor

Debra Parsons, Project Control

Naz Vohra, Graphic Designer

1 Learning and doing

Introduction

For many people learning to do mathematics is difficult, remembering it and applying it appropriately more so, and understanding it even more problematic. This book is designed as a self-study text for people who may have studied mathematics for several years at school but are still not confident that they have sufficient knowledge or understanding of the subject to do what they would like to be able to do in their personal, leisure or work life. You already know, and can do, a great deal of mathematics; this book is about becoming confident in what you can do and extending what you can do by adding meaning, making new connections and becoming more fluent. Revisiting ideas from a slightly different angle and working on them from an adult perspective can reduce anxiety and enable you to move forward with increasing confidence and enjoyment.

Each of the chapters is designed to stand alone, so they can be studied in any order. However, you are advised to work through the rest of this chapter first as it contains some important advice for working on mathematical ideas that are applicable to all the other sections. The chapter will introduce you to a way of working on mathematics which is different from the usual mathematics textbook. It explores some of the reasons why mathematics can seem difficult and some approaches that can help to make learning it a more positive experience. These include ideas for how you might use the rest of the book to meet your particular needs.

Why mathematics can seem difficult

As you work through sections of this book it is worth becoming an active learner – understanding comes from doing and thinking about mathematics, trying to put things in your own words, not just passively reading. This is the purpose of the tasks that occur throughout the book, and you are strongly advised to 'have a go' before starting to read the comments that follow most tasks.

What is mathematics?	Task 1

1   When you think about the word mathematics, which of the following most closely fits your idea of what it means?

   (a) Numbers, symbols and shapes.

(b) A collection of techniques such as how to add fractions, calculate angles, solve equations … .

(c) A toolbox for investigating and solving problems.

(d) Arithmetic, algebra, geometry… .

(e) Counting and measuring, comparison and computing, patterns and properties, analysis and logic.

(f) Abstract study of properties and relationships.

2 Look up a definition of mathematics in a dictionary or encyclopedia. (A source of definitions, and much more, can be found using http://en.wikipedia.org/wiki/Portal:Mathematics – but, as with all web sources, be aware that reliability and accuracy are not assured.)

Comment

The word mathematics encompasses a wide range of ideas and activities – including all of the above. How it is defined tends to depend on whether it is viewed as a tool (for science, engineering, etc.), a way of thinking, or as a study in its own right.

How you view mathematics can affect how you approach learning it. If you think of it as just an unrelated collection of techniques or a series of topics then learning can become a memory test. However, thinking of mathematics as a vast web of related ideas that can provide a way of solving practical or abstract problems can help the process of making connections and developing understanding. It is up to you to make the connections that work for you.

Mathematics can be thought of as a way of thinking or as a language; but for many people the difficulty is how it usually appears when written down. As mathematics has developed, so the means of communicating it through words, symbols and diagrams has become ever more concise and subject to conventions.

To fully understand written mathematics it is essential to be able to unpack the meaning according to context. As in translating a sentence in a foreign language or interpreting a musical score, there is a depth of meaning greater than that of the constituent parts.

Remember, when a word is used in mathematics it sometimes has a different or more precise meaning than the same word used in everyday life; for example, 'sum' is generally used to convey any calculation but in mathematics the 'the sum of' (the Greek letter sigma ($\sum$) as used in spreadsheet programs) signals things that are to be added together. A symbol such as minus (–) can be used in a variety of ways to convey subtly different meanings depending on context, for example:

▶ an operation (a process) as in 7 – 4 (seven subtract, or take away, four);

▶ a comparison as in 7 – 4 = 3 (the difference between seven and four is three);

▶ a directed number as in −7 or sometimes written ⁻7 (negative seven, the additive inverse of 7).

The additive inverse of a number is the number which when added to the original number gives the answer of zero.

Another factor that can seem to add confusion is that the same thing may be represented in different ways, for example $\frac{1}{2}$, 0.5, 50% (or 50/100) are essentially the same number in different forms. Mathematics can also be represented in tables, diagrams, graphs and algebraic expressions. The different representations have developed for a variety of reasons and being able to switch between representations can provide greater insight and make problems simpler to understand and solve.

Being 'stuck'

When you start on a task you may feel that you are not sure what to do or how to do it: you are 'stuck'. Being 'stuck' is a common, and honourable, state when learning or doing mathematics. There are a number of strategies that can make this a positive experience rather than a negative one.

1 Acknowledge that you are stuck, relax and recognise that this is a learning opportunity! Different people develop different strategies for dealing with being stuck. Whatever you do, do not panic.

2 Next try to identify exactly why you are stuck. This process is in effect identifying what you do *know* and what *you want*. Doing this can sometimes be enough for you to see a way of building a bridge between *know* and *want* ... and so become 'unstuck'.

3 Now try and do something about being stuck.

    (a) If the question seems too complicated or too general, try simplifying it in some way. For example, break it down into a sub-set of smaller problems, or rewrite it using simpler numbers or easier words.

    (b) If there does not seem to be enough information, list what else you think you need. (Some tasks may deliberately not have enough information.) Sometimes you may find that you do have the information but it was not in quite the form you expected.

    (c) Tell someone. In trying to explain you may find that you stress and ignore different parts of the problem and so view it in a new light. Even if there is no one around to help, just saying something out loud to yourself can help considerably; saying it 'in your head' is not as powerful.

    (d) Use the solution. Start to read the solution. (In this book the solutions are in the Comments that follow each task.) You may only need to read a little before you can see what is needed and can continue on your own. Or you may need to work through the entire solution before light dawns.

    (e) If you are still stuck, still do not panic – you may need to take a break and do something quite different. Simply freeing your attention can unblock the problem.

(f) If nothing seems to work, skip over the problem area for the moment and look at it again later.

When you have been 'stuck' and then manage to become 'unstuck', think about what happened. The way to make being stuck a positive experience is to notice not only what helped to get you going again, but also what led you to get stuck in the first place. This 'learning from experience' is then available to you for use in future situations.

Making sense of mathematics

There are many strategies that can help you to solve mathematical problems and build up your mathematical knowledge. A useful starting point is trying to make sense of the problem and reviewing what you might already know.

Task 2	What do you notice?

1   Look at the following table, and fill in the next few lines.

2   List all the things you know – or notice – about the items in each column and then in each row (say what you see).

Complete the table

A	B	C	D	E
Row no				
1.	1	1	1×1	1^2
2.	$1 + 3$	4	2×2	2^2
3.	$1 + 3 + 5$		3×3	3^2
4.				
5.				
A whole number of your choice				

Comment

To complete the table you did not need to know very much mathematics as it could be done by following the pattern in each column.

You probably noticed a number of things, perhaps including:

The ellipsis symbol (...) says (is a symbol for) 'and so on'.

▶   going down each column reveals a pattern. For example: column A (1, 2, 3, ...); column B (1, 1 + 3, 1 + 3 + 5, ...); column E (1^2, 2^2, 3^2, ...);

- going across the rows there are various types of symbol, representation and notation. For example in row 2: $1 + 3$, 4, 2×2, 2^2;

- remembering that 3^2 is said 'three-squared' or '3 to the power of 2';

- a moment of surprise – that adding consecutive odd numbers from 1 seems to result in a square number. ('Seems' because at this stage it is a mathematical conjecture – a surmise from a few special cases. So far there is too little information to say whether adding consecutive odd numbers from 1 *always* results in a square number, is generally true. It is, but to be convincing mathematically it is necessary to provide a proof, a topic covered in Chapter 8.)

Completing the table in Task 2 involved using symbols but mathematics is often also represented in diagrams.

Now what do you notice? Task 3

Look at the diagram below. Draw the next diagram in the series. What do you notice that is the same and what is different? Say, and then write down, what you see and any thoughts that arise.

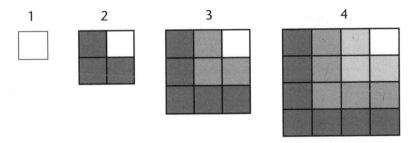

Comment

Focusing attention on what is the same and what is different helps to identify what is special to a particular example and what is general to the set, and can often lead to greater insight.

Each diagram (apart from the 1st) is a square made up of a grid of smaller squares. Diagram 2 is made up of 2×2 squares, diagram 3 of 3×3 squares … .

Doing a physical drawing of the 5th one in the series yourself may have helped to get a sense of the series. You may have drawn a 5×5 grid (why?) and then shaded the smaller squares (did you notice how many you coloured in each shade?), or you may have built up the grid by copying the 4th diagram and then adding smaller squares on the side and bottom (why?), or some other way (why?). Answering the 'whys' will help you capture the order of what you noticed – what you stressed and what you ignored.

It may be difficult to describe the diagrams and thoughts in words at this stage, but trying to describe and articulate can help to get a hold of ideas.

Each diagram is an odd number of smaller squares larger than the previous one.

The diagrams are a geometric representation of the first four rows of the table in Task 2. What do you notice? If you are not sure of this, look back at Task 1 and convince yourself.

The strategy of noticing what is the same and what is different is one that can be useful in making sense in a variety of situations not just ones involving pictures and diagrams. It works because the process encourages the stressing and ignoring of different aspects. Attention is switched back and forth so that the situation can be viewed in new lights and with greater insight.

Visualising a situation is one way of using mental imagery which can include, for example, recall of sounds, feelings, etc. You may have visualised before starting to draw the 5th diagram in Task 3 above. Sometimes mental images take the form of pictures that may not be easy, or helpful, to draw – they may work much better inside your head.

The odd numbers that are added on, the shaded squares, are in an ordered sequence as shown in the table below.

Sequence of odd numbers

Position in sequence	1st	2nd	3rd	4th	5th	...
Value	1	3	5	7	9	...

The diagrams in Task 3 can be visualised as the growing of a square by adding on the sequence of odd numbers represented by small squares. This building up can be described as a mathematical 'doing'.

Task 4	Visualising and representing

Try to visualise the next size square (the 6th) and mentally break it down into the L-shaped pieces which formed it. This can be thought of as 'undoing' the building of the square.

Now try to describe any particular L-shape representation of an odd number in words so that someone else could draw it from your instructions. How might this be used to write down an expression for any odd number?

Looking at special cases is called specialising.

Comment

For example, the 4th odd number (7) might be described as an L-shape made up of two arms, one comprising 4 squares and the other 3 squares (one less than 4), i.e., 4 + 3.

Alternatively, as an L-shape with two arms of 3 squares added to a single square, i.e., 3 + 3 + 1 or (2 × 3) + 1. Notice that 3 is one less than the 4, in the '4th'.

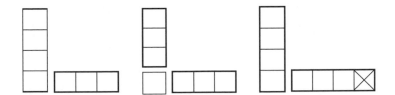

Or as two arms of 4 squares with one square removed (2 × 4) − 1

Any odd number can be represented in the same ways – so one way to find the value of any particular odd number in the sequence is to double the position in the sequence and subtract one.

As has been said, mathematics can be represented in different ways and being able to switch between representations can provide greater insight. In Task 4 above, 'undoing' geometric representations of particular odd numbers (special cases) and then expressing the results numerically in different ways has revealed general patterns of how odd numbers might be 'undone'.

Very often one mathematical process has the effect of undoing another, so that, for example, subtraction undoes addition, halving undoes doubling. Although undoing is often harder than the original doing, thinking in terms of doing and undoing can be very useful in understanding a situation better.

| Doing and undoing | Task 5 |

Using the results of the last task, calculate the following, paying attention to how you solve them.

1 What is the 14th odd number?

2 What position in the sequence of odd numbers has the value of 47?

Comment

Doubling 14 and subtracting 1 gives 27.

This involves 'undoing' the general expression for an odd number. You know that doubling 'something' and subtracting 1 gives 47, what you want is the value of the 'something'. Reasoning suggests that 'double something' must be one more than 47, i.e., 48. Halving 48 (undoing doubling) is 24. Therefore 47 is the 24th odd number.

Notice that not only were the operations 'undone' but the order of doing them was reversed.

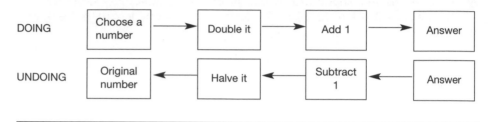

Awareness of the possibility of undoing a mathematical action also allows new questions to be asked and answered, as illustrated in the next task.

Task 6	Undoing squaring

Assuming for the moment that it is certain that the sum ($\sum$) of the first so many odd numbers is that number squared (from Task 2), how many odd numbers need to be added to give a total of 100?

Comment

What is wanted is to find a number that was multiplied by itself (squared) to give 100. The 'doing' was squaring so the 'undoing' is finding the square root ($\sqrt{}$). You almost certainly know that $10 \times 10 = 100$ so $\sqrt{100}$ is 10. So 100 is the sum of the first 10 odd numbers.

Advice on calculator use is given in Chapter 2.

But what if the sum was 361? Unless you happen to know the square root of 361, the sensible way of finding it is to use a calculator or a program such as a spreadsheet. The key or function may be marked as $\boxed{\sqrt{}}$ or $\boxed{\text{sqrt}}$.

Sorting out *what you know* – what the question is about in general as well as the details – and *what you want* is often the key to what you need to do in order to start finding a way to the required solution. This sounds easier than it is in practice; the problem is knowing where to start. It can help to let your mind wander a little, think about whether you are reminded of something similar, and perhaps put the question into different words or conjure up some mental imagery.

Mental imagery need not be visual. Some people find sound an important facet of their powers of imagery – which may be why counting in twos, or fives, or tens can be become very rhythmic. Also reading out loud is a technique which is often helpful in making sense of written mathematics. Mathematical statements can be very condensed so that even a very short statement can carry a lot of meaning and therefore seem difficult to make sense of at first sight.

Let 💭 stand for any whole number. (The 💭 is used to suggest a 'thinks' bubble as in 'think of'.)

Read the following statements out loud and notice what comes to mind before you answer.

What kinds of number are represented by the expressions:

1   2 💭? (double 💭 or 2 times 💭)

2   2 💭 – 1?

Comment

Your thoughts might have gone along the following lines.

1   What do I know? 💭 is any whole number, so particular examples might be 1, 2, 3, or 47 ... (specialising).

    What do I want to make sense of? 2💭, that is 2 × 💭. So specialising again, 2 💭 could be 2, 4, 6, or 94 ... .

    What is the question? What kind of numbers are, for example, 2, 4, 6, or 94 ... ah! – even.

2   Using the same process with 2💭 – 1, you might have caught yourself mentally recalling from an earlier task 'doubling a number and subtracting one' to remind you of odd numbers in general.

Making connections between different types of representations (words – written and said, numbers, symbols, diagrams, expressions, mental imagery ...) can help sense-making and understanding. They can also be aided by specialising (taking particular examples) and generalising (identifying a common pattern).

Think back to see if you have noticed yourself gaining new insight into what mathematics is about and how to make sense of it. What have you learned that is new? Have you recalled or extended something you already knew? How have you been working at the tasks?

Now think about what you want from this book.

Comment

Stopping occasionally to think about what and how you are learning, both in particular and in general, is worthwhile as part of the learning process and to help make best use of time.

Approaches to learning

At the beginning of this chapter you were advised to be an active learner; this inevitably includes having to write things down. There are many ways of keeping notes and how you do so depends on how you learn best and your purpose in studying this book. Separating task work and unfamiliar ideas and definitions is one way, but you may prefer to arrange your work chronologically using highlighters to emphasise key or new ideas. The important thing is to write down thoughts and workings in sufficient detail that your notes will make sense to you when you look back in a few weeks' time.

How the book can be used

The book has been designed so that it can be used in different ways. It can be worked through from beginning to end or you can use the Contents list or the Index to pick out particular chapters or sections that cover the topics you feel you need most. However, if you are not sure what you need and do not have sufficient time to work through it all another approach is possible.

At the end of the book there is a self-assessment chapter. This includes short questions on each main topic, which you are invited to work through and then assess your competence and confidence. Answers are provided and include cross-references to the relevant section of the book. Using this will enable you to make a priority list of topics that you need to learn from scratch, re-learn, revise or practise.

Practice

Unlike many mathematics textbooks this book does not have lots of practice exercises to work through. If you feel the need for more practice, to gain additional fluency, there are many examples available on the web or in GCSE revision books produced by a number of publishers. Just doing lots of examples is not the best way of gaining confidence and understanding – and may not be best use of your time. Doing a few examples and thinking about how to do that type of question in general is likely to be more fruitful. If you can do simple questions on a particular topic but find harder ones more difficult then you need to think about why that may be. What makes a question difficult? It may be longer and so take a little more effort to work out what you know and want, or it may involve additional skills such as manipulating numbers or symbols and that is what you need to practise, the additional skills rather than the particular topic.

Using technology

You will need to use a calculator from time to time. For this level of study it should be a scientific one but access to a simple four-function one would also be useful. Inexpensive models of both types are available from high street stores but you can also find virtual ones free to use or to download from the Internet. Most computers have a built-in simple calculator typically found under programs>accessories>calculator. Once the simple calculator is on screen, you may find that selecting 'view' gives you access to a scientific calculator. Computers also usually have a spreadsheet program as standard.

Other useful programs for enhancing your study of mathematics are readily available and indications of where these might be useful are given in the text. There is a huge range of resources on the Internet and there is a useful Open University maintained portal to some of these at http://skillmath.open.ac.uk/.

A personal dictionary

Another way of being active and marking progress is to create your own 'dictionary' of mathematics including, for example, not so familiar mathematical terms, symbols, representations and connections.

Starting a personal dictionary	Task 9

Look at the Index and then read the section on developing a personalised mathematical dictionary at the very end of the book, and take a few minutes to think about how and where you might create your own dictionary.

Comment

There is good evidence to suggest that mathematical knowledge is at its most secure and usable when the ideas are connected in the mind of the learner. So making connections is yet another important mathematical process in learning and doing mathematics.

This section has introduced a number of words and phrases for aspects of mathematical thinking. These included:

'I know' and 'I want', 'what is the same – what is different', stressing and ignoring, using mental imagery, visualising, doing and undoing, specialising (which can be used to look at particular examples to help make sense of a generalisation or to get a sense of a pattern), generalising (making a reasoned statement applicable to many or all cases), conjecture/conjecturing (forming a possible generalisation on the evidence of a few cases).

These could be the first entries in your mathematical dictionary. You may not want to enter the words in the order they appeared, but to arrange them to reflect connections between them. For example, specialising and generalising might be put together or next to each other.

Furthermore you may wish to leave space after each entry to add to them when new aspects or insights occur – and perhaps date the entries so you can see how understanding has developed over time. Even in this section the notions of doing and undoing have been used both to analyse a diagram (Task 3) and to do and undo a calculation (Task 5).

Notice that almost all the words in the list end in 'ing'. This is because making sense of mathematics is an active process which involves you in doing things. Try to capture that sense of action/activity in your personal definitions in your Mathematical dictionary.

Summary

This chapter has introduced you to a variety of mathematical processes and ways of thinking to aid you as you work through other sections of the book. It has also covered:

▶ why mathematics can seem difficult;

▶ some ways of making sense of mathematics;

▶ approaches to learning mathematics, including being an active learner and different possible ways of using this book.

Further study

Mason, J. (1999) *Learning and Doing Mathematics*, Tarquin Publications. *Learning and Doing Mathematics* provides access to typical modes of mathematical thinking together with advice on how to make use of them when studying.

Mason, J., Burton, L. and Stacey, K. (1985) *Thinking Mathematically*, Prentice Hall. *Thinking Mathematically* offers experiences of mathematical thinking processes which elaborate the ideas in this chapter.

www.nrich.maths.org/ NRICH is a website with a wide range of investigative mathematical problems to work on and discuss with other users.

2 Number

Introduction

This chapter is concerned with numbers and their uses. It concentrates on using numbers as measures and for calculating. The issues raised are as follows.

▶ What is the difference between counting and measuring?

▶ What different kinds of number are there and how are they connected?

▶ What are the different ways of representing numbers?

▶ What are efficient methods of calculating, whether using mental methods, calculators or written methods?

▶ What are the issues involved in calculating with fractions?

The chapter is subdivided into four sections:

▶ how numbers are used;

▶ types of number;

▶ representing numbers;

▶ calculating.

How numbers are used

Numbers are used so commonly and in such diverse ways that their presence is often not noticed. Thinking about how and why numbers are used raises some interesting questions.

▶ Which objects or situations are worth numbering and why?

▶ How do numbers arise?

▶ What sorts of possible numbers are there?

▶ What is done with numbers?

Having an appreciation of the answers to such questions can assist you in working with numbers.

Your knowledge of numbers in everyday life may help you to work through the next tasks.

Think back over the past few days and try to recollect how and where you have seen numbers used. What numbers did you come across and in what contexts? What types of number did you encounter?

Comment

Some examples you may have thought of are shown below.

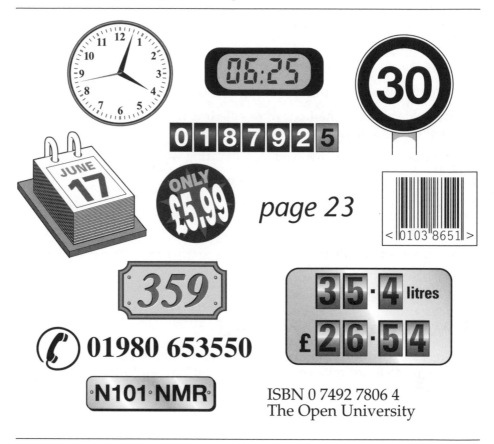

Counting and measuring are the two fundamental ways by which humans have introduced numbers into the world. Counting is used when you need to know how many objects there are, whereas measuring is used when the question 'how much?' is asked. A third use of numbers is for labelling. Objects are often labelled as a result of counting or measuring, but numbers can be used simply as a label that has no special significance other than to identify something.

Look at the examples of ways numbers have been used in Task 10 (look at your own examples and those in the diagram). Sort them into three categories depending on whether they have arisen from counting, measuring or labelling. Add any comment about the particular use of numbers in that context.

Comment

One way the examples of numbers can be sorted depends on their different types of use. This process of sorting and categorising is called classifying.

The table below gives four examples.

Example	Purpose	Comment
House number	Label	Odd and even often give information about position
Speed limit sign	Measure	Units (mph) are omitted
Phone number	label	But can give information about the area
Page number	Count	Sequence gives information about position

Counting

A count is the number of times something has occurred. When the word 'counting' is used you probably think of numbering objects or events 1, 2, 3, 4, ... If you have ever counted a lot of objects you will know how easy it is to lose your place or forget your last number. To avoid this happening people resort to using a tally, a device where one is added to a total automatically (for example, every time a button is pressed or someone walks through a turnstile). Today, much counting is carried out automatically by such tallies: the word count on a word-processor and the total of cars within a pay car-park are examples.

The tally may also be marks on paper, where every fifth mark is drawn across the previous four.

 This makes totalling relatively easy as the tallies can be counted in fives. This and similar methods then require the total to be calculated when the counting has ended.

The purpose of counting is normally to attach a number in order to be able to compare the size of different sets of objects or events. For example, the unemployment or road accident figures can be compared with those from previous years. Sometimes the total produced by counting may be compared with a known value. In the car-park the total will be compared with the total number of spaces; similarly a blood count can be compared with the expected range of values.

As well as being used to compare the relative sizes of sets of objects or events, counting is also used to decide whether a set of things is complete or all there. However, there are occasions when it is not necessary to count every object. For example, many workplaces using tools have specially designed racks to enable them to be seen at a glance whether they are all back in place. There is a one-to-one correspondence between the tools in the set and the number of spaces in the rack.

Counting produces an exact answer, a whole number. For example, there is a definite number of pages in any book, or cars in a car-park. It is this which distinguishes counts from measures.

Measures

When measuring something the question being asked is 'how much?' in order to make a either an absolute or relative comparison. Whereas counts answer the question 'how many? and require only discrete whole numbers, other measures can also use continuous scales and involve fractions, decimals, percentages and ratios.

Chapter 3 also covers the nature of measures including proportion in greater detail and Chapter 4 considers statistical comparison.

The use of numbers in varying situations is not clear cut. For example, ordinal numbers (1st, 2nd, 3rd …) are labels but indicate relative position, but the relationship between the numbers is different to that between the fixed interval of hours of the day (1 o'clock, 2 o'clock). Number symbols used in these different ways have differing properties and the taxonomy of these is covered in Chapter 3.

However, in pure mathematics the counting numbers have developed into a range of apparently different numbers that have common properties. The relationship between these numbers is discussed in the next section.

Number

This section looks at the different types of 'pure' number, the names given to them and the relationships between them.

Task 12	Numb and number

How many different types of number on this list do you already know? Could you explain them to someone else or give an example of their use?

counting numbers	integers	decimals
rational numbers	irrational numbers	real numbers
natural numbers	whole numbers	fractions
positive numbers	negative numbers	complex numbers

Comment

Historically, it took many centuries to invent and then to sort out the different kinds of number and their properties. It is possible that you can explain some of these types of number but are not sure how they link together.

The history of number and number systems is a fascinating topic in its own right. There are many resources available on the Web.

The counting numbers

The smallest counting number is usually taken to be 1. One way to visualise the counting numbers is to imagine a blank line with the counting numbers as stepping stones, starting with 1 and going on for ever. The number line below shows the steps going to the right.

Since 1 can be added to any number, potentially the counting numbers go on for ever. Counting in English words can eventually run into difficulty, requiring words like *billion*, *trillion*, *quadrillion*, *quintillion*, and so on. With written numbers, however, the principle of place value (together with the number symbols 0–9) is completely versatile: using these digits in combination *any* counting number can be written down.

A billion is generally taken to mean a thousand million. This was its original usage in the USA, whereas in Britain it was a million million.

Other names that are sometimes used for the counting numbers are the natural numbers and the whole numbers. Both of these uses can be confusing, partly because it is not always clear whether the number zero (or 'nought') is included or not. It is probably best to use 'natural numbers' as an alternative to 'counting numbers', and use 'whole numbers' when you want to include zero.

Extending   **Task 13**

Another way of thinking of the counting numbers is that they are the ones which can be produced on a calculator just using the keys marked 1, 2, ..., 8, 9 and the ⊞ and ⊟ keys.

What other numbers can you produce using the ⊟ key instead of the ⊞ key?

Comment

Using the subtraction key can lead to zero and negative numbers.

The integers

The set of integers (which are also sometimes referred to, ambiguously, as the whole numbers) comprises zero and the counting numbers (this time

---

thought of as the positive whole numbers), and also the negative whole numbers (⁻1, ⁻2, ⁻3, …). A helpful image here is to picture a mirror placed at the zero of the whole numbers; the negative integers are then the mirror images of the corresponding positive integers.

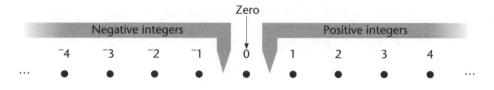

Decimals, fractions and rational numbers

The counting numbers were extended to the integers by using subtraction. Similarly, the counting numbers can be further extended using division. For example:

What number is produced by carrying out the division 3 ÷ 5?

Three possible answers are:

3 ÷ 5 gives the decimal (fraction) 0.6;

3 ÷ 5 gives the (bar) fraction $\frac{3}{5}$;

3 ÷ 5 gives the rational number $\frac{3}{5}$.

These three answers all represent the same number. Rational numbers are an attempt to make the number line like a continuous line rather than a series of stepping stones. On the number line $\frac{3}{5}$ will go between 0 and 1. The decimal 0.6 is a different way of representing the same rational number.

The rational number $\frac{3}{5}$ arose from the division 3 ÷ 5, but this is not the only division that gives this number. The word 'rational' comes from ratio, which involves expressing the relationship between two numbers (see Chapter 3).

Task 14	More divisions

Write down several more divisions that will give the answer 0.6. Think how you might generate an unlimited number of such divisions.

Comment

Some possible answers are:

6 ÷ 10, 12 ÷ 20, 30 ÷ 50, 12 000 ÷ 20 000.

It is worth thinking about methods for creating divisions to give the same answer. The answers above suggest some methods. Can you use them to create more divisions? Can you produce a division that is unlikely to be produced by anyone else?

Each of the fractions created from the divisions given in Task 14,

$$\frac{6}{10}, \quad \frac{12}{20}, \quad \frac{30}{50}, \quad \frac{12\,000}{20\,000},\quad\text{\textendash}$$

represents the same rational number, the same point on the number line. They are called equivalent fractions and the underlying number is called the rational number. When naming a rational number it is usual to give either the decimal or the fraction involving the smallest numbers – in this case, 0.6 or $\frac{3}{5}$. The choice between using fractions or decimals depends on the need to make a calculation easier or to make communication clearer. When using a calculator it is likely that using decimals is more efficient.

Dividing any whole number by another produces a rational number. For example, starting with 1 and 2, dividing 1 by 2 gives $\frac{1}{2}$, a new point on the number line that is equidistant between 0 and 1.
Of course, the division could be performed the other way round: 2 divided by 1 gives the result 2 ($\frac{2}{1} = 2$) which is a whole number. This demonstrates that the integers can also be thought of as rational numbers, since they can be produced by dividing two whole numbers – themselves and 1.

Dividing one integer by another appears to produce a system of numbers which fills every possible point on the number line. For example, 2.1 and 2.2 can be obtained as $\frac{21}{10}$ and $\frac{22}{10}$ respectively; it is possible to think of a rational number lying between them: 2.13 or 2.17, perhaps. This can be achieved by dividing by 100 instead of 10:

$$\frac{213}{100} = 2.13 \quad \text{and} \quad \frac{217}{100} = 2.17.$$

By a similar process, a rational number between 2.13 and 2.14 can be found by choosing 1000 as the divisor:

$$\frac{2136}{100} = 2.136.$$

This process can be carried out between any pair of decimals.

Fractions and decimals are not different types of number, but different ways of representing rational numbers.

$\frac{2}{1}$ is the reciprocal of $\frac{1}{2}$

Filling the gaps   Task 15

Create numbers between 4.1722 and 4.1723 and between 4.1729 and 4.173. Try to imagine the numbers on your number line.

Comment
Between the two adjacent numbers 4.1722 and 4.1723 nine new numbers can be fitted by this process: 4.172 21, 4.172 22, 4.172 23, ... , 4.172 29. The process is completely general. On a number line composed of rational numbers, the gap between any two numbers can be filled with more rational numbers by increasing the divisor by a multiple of 10.

Here is a number line with some rational numbers.

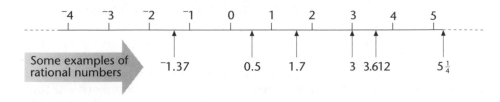

Some examples of rational numbers

‾1.37   0.5   1.7   3 3.612 $5\frac{1}{4}$

Ordering fractions and decimals

It is often convenient to express fractions as decimals since ordering fractions can be quite difficult. For example, not many people could say immediately which of $\frac{8}{11}$ and $\frac{7}{9}$ is the larger. Decimals, because they use the place-value system, can be ordered more readily in size, but there are features of ordering decimals that many people find confusing. You may have fallen into some of these traps yourself in the past. See if you recognise the possible confusions in the following task.

Task 16	Ordering decimals

Write the following decimals in order, smallest first:

(a) 0.07, 0.23, 0.1

(b) 0.735, 0.74

(c) ‾3.75, ‾2.84

In each case give a reason why someone might give the wrong answer.

Comment

(a) 0.07, 0.1, 0.23 is correct. Someone might ignore the decimal point and write 0.1, 0.07, 0.23 because they see only the 1, 7 and the 23 and put those in order.

(b) 0.735, 0.74 is correct. Some people believe 0.74 is smaller than 0.735 because it contains fewer digits

(c) ‾3.75, ‾2.84 is correct. Someone might believe that ‾2.84 is smaller because, with the positive numbers 2.84 and 3.75, 2.84 *is* smaller.

It has been suggested that some of these mistakes may partly be due to the overemphasis on using money as a means of introducing decimals. For example, £1.25 is said 'one pound twenty-five', whereas 1.25 is said 'one point two five'. A very common error is to say 'one point twenty-five' for the decimal.

Infinite decimals

If you attempted to find which of $\frac{8}{11}$ and $\frac{7}{9}$ is the larger fraction by carrying out the divisions on a calculator, you would get:

$\frac{8}{11} = 0.727\ 272\ 727$ and $\quad \frac{7}{9} = 0.777\ 777\ 778$

(The number of digits shown depends upon your calculator.)

In each case the answer is an infinite recurring (repeating) decimal. All rational numbers produce a decimal which is either terminating or recurring. So, for example:

$\frac{1}{3} = 0.333\ 333\ 333\ ...$, $\frac{41}{333} = 0.123\ 123\ 123\ 123\ ...$, and $\frac{27}{250} = 0.108$.

There are also infinite decimals that neither terminate nor recur; and which cannot be obtained by dividing two integers. These numbers are called the irrational numbers (i.e., the 'not-rationals') and fill the gaps in the number line left between the rational numbers. They include numbers like $\sqrt{2}$ (the number which when multiplied by itself gives 2), $\sqrt{5}$ and so on. Amazingly, the decimal expansion of $\sqrt{2}$ never repeats itself:

1.414 213 562 373 095 048 801 688 724 209 698 078 569 671 875 376
948   073 176 679 737 990 732 478 462 107 038 850 387 534 327 641
572   735 013 846 230 912 297 024 924 836 055 850 737 212 644 121
497   099 935 831 413 222 665 927 505 592 755 799 950 501 152 782
060   571 470 109 ... (and on and on).

Another irrational number is π. Thus π is not equal to $\frac{22}{7}$ (a fraction that is a close, but smaller approximation and is a recurring decimal).

π can be defined either as the area of a circle whose radius is one unit, or as the ratio of the circumference to the diameter of any circle.

Real numbers

The numbers that include the rationals and irrationals are called the real numbers.

Despite the variety of names, any real number can be thought of as a point lying somewhere on the number line.

There are more types of number, for example, complex numbers. These are based on $\sqrt{-1}$ which has the symbol i (for imaginary number). Complex numbers are ones which use both real numbers and i ($2 + 3i$ is an example). Although such numbers can seem strange, they have many practical applications in engineering and science, and are used to create the popular pictures of chaos and fractals. This book does not cover complex numbers but it is worth knowing that such numbers exist.

All the above types of 'pure' number share particular properties (but have additional ones of their own).

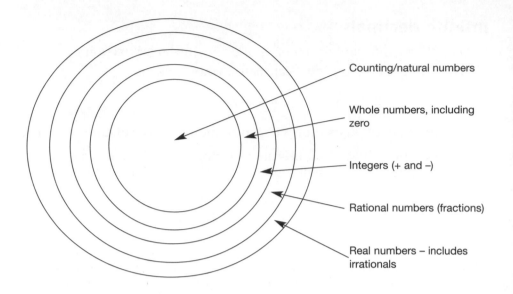

Counting/natural numbers

Whole numbers, including zero

Integers (+ and –)

Rational numbers (fractions)

Real numbers – includes irrationals

Representing numbers

Common ways of representing numbers are:

▶ the place-value system (the usual way of representing whole numbers and decimals);

▶ fractions and percentage notation;

▶ index notation;

▶ scientific notation.

These are each examined in this section.

The place-value system

The Indian–Arabic (or Hindu–Arabic) system most generally used in the western world has ten numerals (0, 1, 2, 3, 4, 5, 6, 7, 8, 9) which are combined in a place-system structure.

The name of the symbol 6 in English is 'six', but the meaning changes depending on its position such as:

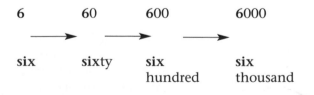

6	60	600	6000
six	sixty	six hundred	six thousand

Ten thousands	Thousands	Hundreds	Tens	Units	tenths	hundredths	thousandths
10 000	1 000	100	10	1	0.1	0.01	0.001

The place-value system extends to decimals.

Fractions and percentages

Rational numbers represented as quotients ($\frac{\text{numerator}}{\text{denominator}}$) are variously referred to as fractions, common (vulgar) fractions, and bar fractions.

Are percentages ('per-hundred') fractions? Are they decimals ... or something else? An extract from a newspaper report on changes in shopping reads as follows.

> Total sales by butchers have slipped in every year of this decade; last year's total of £1.7 billion is 62 per cent of that of 1990. ... The top 10 chain [stores] account for half the total sales of all 775 companies in the report and two-fifths of all shop-spending in Britain.
>
> (Source: *Guardian*, 5 May 1998)

This mixture of numbers written as decimals, percentages and fractions is very common in the media; it is useful to be able to change from one form to another.

Percentages are often thought of as fractions, so 45% is $\frac{45}{100}$. But because the denominator of the fraction is hundredths, it is usually more appropriate, especially when using a calculator, to think of percentages as decimals in disguise: 45% = 0.45. This means that finding a percentage of something is the same as multiplying by a decimal.

A label that reads '60% cotton and 40% polyester' means that $\frac{60}{100}$ or $\frac{6}{10}$ (0.6), is cotton while $\frac{40}{100}$, or $\frac{4}{10}$ (0.4), is polyester.

Fractions and decimals can both be seen as the result of a division, and so moving from fractions to percentages is best done by changing the fraction to a decimal and then changing the decimal to a percentage.

$\frac{3}{4} = 0.75 = \frac{75}{100} = 75\%$

Sometimes it will not be an exact amount. $0.8333 \approx 0.83 = 83\%$ (rounded to the nearest 1%).

Index notation

Using power notation for numbers, writing numbers as 5^2, 5^3 and so on, is just a shorthand form, but an efficient one. For example, multiplying 5s together successively gives:

$5 \times 5 = 25$ $5 \times 5 \times 5 = 125$ $5 \times 5 \times 5 \times 5 = 625$
$5 \times 5 \times 5 \times 5 \times 5 = 3125$ etc.

Using the shorthand notation this becomes:

$5^2 = 25$ $5^3 = 125$ $5^4 = 625$ $5^5 = 3125$

In this example, 5 is the base number and the superscript number at the top right indicates how many of these base numbers have been multiplied together. This superscript number is called the power or index or exponent.

The term 5^5 is read as 'five to the power 5' and 5^4 as 'five to the power 4'. Although 5^3 could be read as 'five to the power 3' it is usually said 'five cubed'; it may help you to remember this by relating it to a cube in 3D (three-dimensional) space. Similarly 5^2 is usually read as 'five squared' and relates to a square in 2D (two-dimensional) space.

The powers 2, 3 and 4 in 5^2, 5^3, 5^4 are all counting numbers. However, the value of this shorthand arises when the index number is extended to negative and fractional numbers. The extension to negative numbers is looked at here. The original numbers are:

Index	2	3	4	5
Power of 5	25	125	625	3125

Imagine reading from right to left: the numbers in the top row are going down in 1s; the numbers in the bottom row are being divided by 5. If the top row is extended leftwards the table would read:

$^-3$	$^-2$	$^-1$	0	1	2	3	4	5
$\frac{1}{125}$	$\frac{1}{125}$	$\frac{1}{5}$	1	5	25	125	625	3125

This extension gives:

$$5^1 = 5 \qquad 5^0 = 1 \qquad 5^{-1} = \tfrac{1}{5} \qquad 5^{-2} = \tfrac{1}{25} \qquad 5^{-3} = 1\tfrac{1}{125}$$

Notice that:

$$5^{-2} = \tfrac{1}{5^2} \qquad 5^{-3} = \tfrac{1}{5^3} \quad \text{and so on.}$$

In this process of extending a mathematical idea, the pattern of numbers in the table has been preserved, but where previously $5^3 = 5 \times 5 \times 5$ could be said as 'three 5s multiplied together', it is not possible to think of 5^{-3} in the same way as 'negative three 5s multiplied together'. Usually, when extending a mathematical idea, some aspects are preserved and others lost.

This notation does not just apply to powers of 5 but to powers of any number. It is especially used with powers of 10 because 10 is the basis for the place-value system.

Thousands	Hundreds	Tens	Units	tenths	hundredths	thousandths
1000	100	10	1	0.1	0.01	0.001
10^3	10^2	$10'$	10^0	10^{-1}	10^{-2}	10^{-3}

Scientific notation

A simple ('four-function') calculator will have a display that shows probably eight digits on it. So the largest number that can be entered is 99 999 999, and the smallest is ⁻99 999 999. The number closest to 0 (apart from 0 itself) will be 0.000 000 1. Calculations involving bigger numbers or ones closer to zero need a scientific calculator which shows numbers written in scientific notation (also known as standard form).

Using this notation, numbers can be expressed in a particularly neat form as illustrated by the following examples:

$$250 = 2.5 \times 10^2$$
$$25 = 2.5 \times 10^1$$
$$2.5 = 2.5 \times 10^0$$
$$0.25 = 2.5 \times 10^{-1}$$

In general,

any number = (number between 1 and 10) × (power of 10)

Note that a scientific calculator:

▶ may possibly display numbers with ten or more digits;

▶ will also display larger (and smaller) numbers using scientific notation.

Big numbers	Task 17

What answer would you expect if you find the square of 20 million (i.e., multiply 20 million by itself)? How many noughts should the answer have?

If you have a scientific calculator available, enter 20 000 000 and then press the 'square' key, usually marked $\boxed{x^2}$.

Comment

You should find that the calculator will display 4.0 14, or perhaps 4.0 E14 where E stands for 'exponent'. (Different calculators may display the answer in various ways.) These both mean:

4.0×10^{14} or 400 000 000 000 000

Try some more calculations which involve the use of huge numbers.

A scientific calculator will enable you to extend the end of the number line up to something like 9.9999×10^{99}. This is quite a big number, but the space for numbers beyond is still infinitely large! However, most scientific calculators will helpfully display 'ERROR' if you venture into parts of the number line that they are not programmed to reach.

Methods of using your calculator constant facility are explained on page 29.

Small numbers very close to zero can also be formed in this way. For example, set up your calculator constant facility to divide by 10, enter a simple starting value, say 43, and then repeatedly press the $\boxed{=}$ key. Watch carefully how, after about nine presses, the display suddenly jumps into scientific notation and you see 4.3 ⁻08, 4.3 ⁻09, ... Extending this principle, the smallest number greater than zero that this calculator can handle will be 1.0 ⁻99. There is still a very small gap between this number and zero. However, even within this extremely small region, an infinity of numbers exist!

A version of roughly what the scientific calculator number line might look like is shown below. It assumes a model with only an eight-digit display.

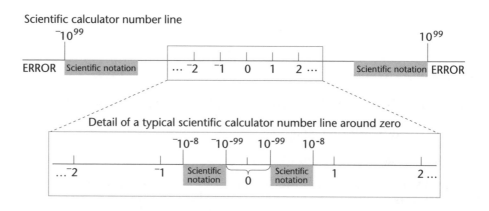

Scientific calculator number line

Detail of a typical scientific calculator number line around zero

It is worth while spending some time studying this diagram and being quite precise about what the significant boundaries mean and where they lie. For example, can you distinguish between the very large negative number, ⁻10⁹⁹, and the very small positive number, 10⁻⁹⁹?

This would be a good point to ensure that you know how to enter different types of numbers directly onto your calculator.

Task 18	Entering numbers

Check that you know how to enter different types of number on your calculator.

(a) Negative numbers – can you get your calculator to work out ⁻3 x ⁻5?

(b) Can you enter and use decimals?

(c) If you have a scientific calculator, do you know how to enter a number such as 9.46×10^{12} (the number of kilometres in one light-year)?

Calculating

The 'four rules'

The concepts of addition, subtraction, multiplication and division are complex abstract ideas which are interrelated.

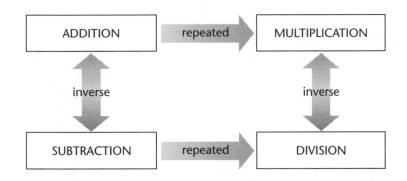

Since concepts are, by definition, abstract, they cannot be expressed precisely in words or diagrams. However, aspects can be illustrated by example.

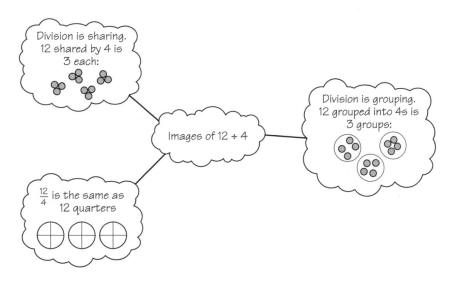

The various ways of doing calculations involving the four rules can be categorised by the different means used:

▶ mental methods;

▶ methods using a calculator;

▶ written methods.

Consider the following calculations

(a) 361 – 261   (b) 361 × 261   (c) 361 + 261

What method would you use for each of these: mental, written, or a calculator?

Comment

The methods you use will depend on how adept you are at each of them. You may have worked out 361 – 261 = 100 mentally, whereas it is more likely that you used a calculator to work out 361 × 261 = 94 221. When working out 361 + 261 = 622 it is possible that you used any one of the methods or indeed all three. It is quite common for people to use a combination of all three methods.

When you are manipulating numbers you are aiming for fluency as well as accuracy, but not necessarily great speed. There are some skills and strategies that help when using each of these methods.

This section looks at the various methods of calculating – mental methods, ones using a calculator, and written methods. It then discusses calculating with fractions, decimals and percentages. For such calculations, most people use a mixture of methods depending on the actual numbers involved.

Mental methods

In recent times there has been a much increased emphasis on mental arithmetic in schools, and most adults sometimes use mental methods for informal calculations where the numbers are simple or a calculator is not to hand. Quick recall of number facts and fast mental calculation has been taken to be evidence of understanding and high mathematical ability. Equally, poor recall and slow calculation has been taken as evidence of low ability. But these are very dubious assertions.

This section helps you think about the methods you use when calculating mentally (you may find that you use more than you are aware of). Useful mental calculating strategies are then looked at.

There are several important aspects to mental calculation.

▶ For any mental calculation there can be a wide variety of methods – some are more efficient than others for *particular numbers*, while some are more efficient for the *particular person* doing the calculation. Also, there is variation in the need for accuracy, determined by the purpose of the calculation in the context in which it arose.

▶ There is a need to understand ('have a feel for') numbers and operations in order to devise an appropriate method. But, mental methods can be shared; they do not need to be reinvented by every individual.

> Mental methods commonly take a different form from the standard written methods.

Use the following task as a way of finding out some of the methods you use.

Buying stamps

Mentally work out how much it would cost to buy the following postage stamps (do each part without using the solution to a previous one). Think about what method you use.

(a) 50 at 28p each
(b) 27 at 50p each
(c) 25 at 75p each
(d) 28 at 75p each

Comment

Did you always use the same method? If not, why not? The following are some which you might have used for part (d):

> $75p = £\frac{3}{4}$, $28 \times \frac{3}{4} = 28 \div 4 \times 3 = 7 \times 3 = 21$, so £21

> $2 \times 75p = £1.50$, $14 \times 1.50 = (10 \times 1.50) + (4 \times 1.50) = 15 + 6 = 21$, £21

> $20 \times 0.75 = 15$, $8 \times 0.75 = 6$, $15 + 6 = 21$, £21

> 2 stamps cost £1.50 so 4 cost £3; 28 is 7 groups of 4, $7 \times £3 = £21$

In some of these calculations the units (£) were omitted for brevity and only put in at the end – great care needs to be taken when working like this, particularly when more than one unit is involved.

Mental strategies

With mental calculations there are no set methods – what you use depends on your personal strategies and the actual numbers.

This creates difficulties for some people who feel lost without a standard method to hold on to. However, there is plenty of evidence that you can improve your mental arithmetic by being more aware of strategies you use and deliberately trying new ones. For example, one strategy is to break down a number into parts that are easier to deal with. This strategy is often used by people who can work out VAT (value added tax) in their heads. At the time of writing, VAT is payable at 17.5%. At first glance this appears to be a bizarre amount. But you can break down 17.5% as follows:

$$17.5\% = 10\% + 5\% + 2.5\%$$

To work out 17.5% of £48 you would calculate these three percentages (10% is straightforward, and the others are each half of the previous one) and add them:

You use a method with particular numbers, but a strategy is more like a generalisation of a collection of methods.

$$17.5\% \text{ of } £48 = £4.80 + £2.40 + £1.20 = £8.40$$

Try this method on £64.

You may have found that you had difficulty in 'holding' three different figures in your head. Mental methods do not need to be entirely 'in the head'; it is often useful to jot down intermediate numbers.

Here is another example: 506 – 309.

Method 1: Subtracting 300 from 506 leaves 206. Taking 9 from 206 leaves 197.

Method 2: Subtracting 300 from 500 leaves 200. Taking 6 from 9 leaves 3. Taking 3 from 200 leaves 197.

Method 3: Make the 309 up to 400 which gives 91, then add 100, then add the 6, giving 197.

These three methods share a common feature in that they work with the bigger numbers, the hundreds, before the units. In the standard written methods, the rule is to start with the units for addition, subtraction and multiplication, but not for division!

Below are some common strategies that you might use.

Addition and subtraction strategies

▶ Count on or back in repeated steps of 10, 2 or 5.

▶ Identify near doubles and adjust.

▶ Separate into tens and units and add tens first.

▶ Add/subtract 9, 19, 29, ... or 11, 21, 31, ... by adding/subtracting 10, 20, 30, ... then adjusting by 1.

▶ Add several small numbers and look for pairs that total 10.

Multiplication and division strategies

▶ To multiply by 10, shift digits one place to the left.

▶ To divide by 10, shift digits one place to the right.

▶ Use the relationship between multiplication and division as inverses.

▶ Use related facts of doubling and halving.

▶ Use closely related facts already known.

▶ Split numbers into parts that are easily dealt with.

Calculators

While it is possible to use calculators for simple calculations, they are not always the most efficient method. For example, the calculation 22 + 23 requires six key presses to get the answer:

2 2 [+] 2 3 [=]

Doing a sum like this mentally is usually faster than using a calculator; you need to use your judgement about when to reach for a calculator.

Many people are sometimes unsure exactly which keys to press to work out a calculation: for example, £12.99 less 5% discount. This is partly because they are unsure how to use particular kinds of keys, and partly because calculators do not always give the outcome you might expect. This section examines the following issues:

▶ unexpected answers on calculators;

▶ calculator logics;

▶ the use of the calculator constant facility.

The next task draws your attention to some of the features of calculator operation. The intention is to raise issues through your being surprised, perhaps, at the answers the calculator gives.

Calculator key sequences are shown with the numbers in bold and the operation keys in a box.

Guess and press	Task 21

(a) Look at each key sequence below. Before you use a calculator, *write down* what answer you would expect it to produce on the calculator display.

(b) For each key sequence, press the keys in the given order on your calculator and write down the result you actually got. Clear the calculator display before moving to the next key sequence.

(c) Try the activity with a different type of calculator. (Remember virtual calculators are available on the web.)

Although this task can be carried out on your own, it is better done with a small group of people working and discussing together.

Some calculators do not have a $\boxed{=}$ key but have $\boxed{\text{ENTER}}$ or $\boxed{\text{EXE}}$.

	Key sequence	Guess	Calculator 1	Calculator 2
(i)	**7** $\boxed{\div}$ **4**			
(ii)	**3** $\boxed{\div}$ **4** $\boxed{=}$			
(iii)	**2** $\boxed{\div}$ **4** $\boxed{=}$			
(iv)	**2** $\boxed{+}$ **3** $\boxed{\times}$ **4** $\boxed{=}$			
(v)	**2** $\boxed{+}$ $\boxed{+}$ **3** $\boxed{=}$			
(vi)	**2** $\boxed{+}$ $\boxed{+}$ **3** $\boxed{=}$ $\boxed{=}$			

Comment

Some examples of the sorts of issues that this task was designed to raise are given below.

(i) 7 $\boxed{\div}$ 4 As written, most calculators will show 4. Two points arising from this are, first, that most calculator key sequences require the press of $\boxed{=}$ or $\boxed{\text{EXE}}$ to complete them, and second, that it is worth clearly distinguishing between a textbook 'sum' and a calculator key sequence.

(ii) **3** $\boxed{\div}$ **4** $\boxed{=}$ and (iii) **2** $\boxed{\div}$ **3** $\boxed{=}$ Although the first division (3 ÷ 4) gives an exact answer, the second (2 ÷ 3) produces a string of digits which (in theory) goes on for ever. This reveals two interesting features of your calculator. First, does it 'round' the final digit up to 7, or does it 'cut' the string, leaving a 6 as the final digit displayed? Second, how many digits can your calculator display - eight, ten or twelve?

(iv) **2** $\boxed{+}$ **3** $\boxed{\times}$ **4** $\boxed{=}$ This sequence will produce the answer 14 or 20, depending on the operating system of the calculator you are using. This is an important thing to know and is explained more fully in the next task, 'Calculator logic'.

(v) **2** $\boxed{+}$ $\boxed{+}$ **3** $\boxed{=}$ and (vi) **2** $\boxed{+}$ $\boxed{+}$ **3** $\boxed{=}$ $\boxed{=}$ These sequences are likely to raise questions about the calculator's constant facility. The constant facility is such a useful feature of calculators that it is also explored later in this section.

One of the problems of working with calculators is that they do not all work in the same way. You have to get to know your particular calculator and its nuances.

Task 22	Calculator logic

Imagine that someone asks you to do the following calculation in your head. Read it out loud before doing it.

What is 2-plus-3 (pause) times 4?

Now try the following calculation, again reading it out loud first.

What is 2 plus (pause) 3-times-4?

Finally, here is an exercise in algebra to try.

Find the value of the expression $2 + 3a$, when $a = 4$.

Comment

It is likely that for the first sentence, when read as written above, you will produce the answer 20. For the second calculation, although the basic words are the same, the answer is less certain. If you read the '3-times-4' part all in a rush, as written above, the answer 14 may seem more appropriate (i.e., as 2 + 12).

The algebra example, when the a is replaced by 4, produces the same calculation, namely 2 + 3 × 4. This time the answer of 14 is inescapable, because the rules of algebra dictate that the multiplication of 3 x 4 must be completed before the 2 is added.

So, what will your calculator make of 2 + 3 x 4?

Calculators, unfortunately, are not programmed to interpret dramatic pauses and changes of intonation when given instructions to perform a calculation. They will simply calculate according to the rules with which they have been programmed.

Most calculators have either an arithmetic (pronounced arith**me**tic, with the stress on the third syllable) or an algebraic operating system. Calculators which perform the operations from left to right in the order in which they are keyed in (i.e., ones which will give the answer 20 to the above sequence) are said to have an 'arithmetic operating system'. Calculators which conform to algebraic rules, such as that multiplication and division must be performed before addition and subtraction (i.e., which will give the answer 14 to the above sequence) are said to have an 'algebraic operating system'.

Most basic calculators are often termed 'four-function' machines. These usually have arithmetic logic (but not always) and will carry out addition, subtraction, multiplication and division of numbers (the four functions referred to in the name). On the other hand, scientific calculators tend to conform to an algebraic operating system. Some, but not all, calculators on mobile phones also have an algebraic operating system.

The calculator constant facility
An especially useful feature of a calculator is the 'constant' facility – the method by which you can carry out repeat operations.

The constant facility is a way of setting up the calculator to do a particular calculation and, thereafter, it will continue to perform the same calculation each time the $=$ key is pressed. The constant facility can be thought of as a form of 'function machine', where you input a number into the calculator, press $=$ to apply the function, and the output value then appears in the display.

Almost all calculators have a constant facility, but unfortunately they do not all operate with the constant in the same way. The two most common methods of setting up and operating the constant, the 'automatic' and the 'double-press' constant are described below. Check which way works for your machine. If neither works, track down the calculator's manual and see whether it can be set up by some other means (for example, some calculator constants are based on a key marked K).

This will enable you to check whether your calculator has an automatic or a double-press constant.

(a) Carry out this sequence:

For calculators with a double-press constant, this key sequence should produce the 2 times table. (Many calculators show a small 'K' in the display to indicate that the constant has been activated.) For calculators with an automatic constant, '2' will remain in the display.

Carry out this sequence:

8 $+$ 2 $=$ $=$ $=$ ...

If successive presses of $=$ have the effect of changing the number on the display, then you know that your calculator has an automatic constant facility. Such calculators will produce a sequence of numbers. (Other calculators will show '10' on the display throughout.)

(Only if you have a calculator with an automatic constant.) There is more than one type of automatic constant. You need to discover whether the constant operation is applied to the number *before* the operation each time (i.e., the 8) or the number *after* it (the 2). This needs to be checked out carefully for any new calculator you use, as it varies from model to model. To find out which type you have, carry out the following sequences:

8 $-$ 2 $=$ $=$ $=$ ...

8 $\times$ 2 $=$ $=$ $=$ ...

Written methods

Written methods of calculation are useful when:

- calculations are too complex to be done entirely mentally, and a calculator is not available;

- when the process of calculation needs to be communicated to someone else.

These occur much less frequently than they used to. The 'standard written methods' were devised to enable clerks, who had no other aids to calculation, to carry out calculations efficiently. 'Efficiency' involved writing down as little as possible, while still leaving the intermediate calculations apparent and hence available for subsequent checking. Today, the standard written methods are used remarkably little in the adult world. This may be because they are so difficult to learn and remember, but it is more likely because they are seldom the most appropriate to use. You probably find that you use mainly mental methods, informal writing down and the calculator.

Written methods for the four rules on whole numbers are not discussed here as they are likely to be familiar to you. One of the aspects of whole numbers where you may use a mix of written and calculator methods is in finding their factors.

Finding multiples of a number is straightforward. The multiples of 6, say, are just those numbers into which 6 divides exactly: 6, 12, 18, 24, 30, ... They are the numbers in the 6 times table. Undoing the process – finding what numbers divide exactly into a given number; that is, finding the factors – is not so easy. In fact, for large numbers it is extremely difficult, which is why it is used as a basis for creating codes that are difficult to break, for example making online financial transactions secure.

It is not obvious what the factors are of, say, 2093. There are actually eight numbers which divide 2093 exactly: 1, 7, 13, 23, 91, 161, 299, 2093. How could you find such numbers? There are two key aspects to be considered.

▶ Factors occur in pairs: if 7 divides into 2093 exactly it must pair with another number that also divides into 2093. In fact, 7 × 299 = 2093.

▶ Some of the factors are prime numbers. The rest are made up of those prime numbers.

Prime numbers are those that have just two numbers that will divide them: 1 and the number itself. So 2, 3, 5, 7, 11, 13 are all prime numbers. 1 is not a prime number as it only has one divisor.

For 2093, the eight numbers pair as follows:

1 × 2093, 7 × 299, 13 × 161, 23 × 91

The prime numbers here are 7, 13, 23. The other numbers each have other factors:

91 = 7 × 13, 161 = 7 × 23, 299 = 13 × 23

Notice that these factors are each made by multiplying together prime factors. This example suggests a method for finding the factors of any number. This is demonstrated below with the number 476.

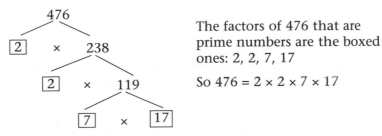

The factors of 476 that are prime numbers are the boxed ones: 2, 2, 7, 17

So 476 = 2 × 2 × 7 × 17

This method is usually called 'producing a factor tree'.

These routines for written calculations are referred to as 'standard written methods', 'standard written algorithms', or 'traditional pencil-and-paper methods'. Examples are the 'decomposition' method for subtraction, and the method of 'long multiplication'.

There is an infinite number of prime numbers.

Find the prime factors of:

(a) 72

(b) 855

Comment

The prime factors are:

(a) $72 = 2 \times 2 \times 2 \times 3 \times 3$

(b) $855 = 3 \times 3 \times 5 \times 19$

Calculating with fractions

When calculations involve fractions you are unlikely to use only written methods. Most people use a mixture of written, mental and calculator methods, depending on the numbers involved.

How would you carry out the following calculation?

$$\frac{1}{4} + \frac{1}{3}$$

Comment

You were probably taught this method at school:

$$\frac{1}{4} + \frac{1}{3} = \frac{3}{12} + \frac{4}{12} = \frac{7}{12}$$

For this method you need to use equivalent fractions – which you saw on the number line. To add or subtract fractions each denominator (number under the bar) must be the same. So:

$$\frac{1}{4} = \frac{2}{8} = \frac{3}{12} = \dots \text{ and } \frac{1}{3} = \frac{2}{6} = \frac{3}{9} = \frac{4}{12} = \dots$$

Many people find the addition and subtraction of fractions cumbersome. If the question was more complicated then it would make sense to use a calculator that can add fractions. In reality it is likely that the fractions will be changed to decimals before they are manipulated. But this can introduce an inaccuracy in the calculation when the decimal forms of the numbers are infinite repeating decimals. For example:

$$\frac{3}{7} + \frac{1}{3} = \frac{16}{21}$$

but, in decimals, a four-function calculator gives:

$$0.428\ 571\ 4 + 0.333\ 333\ 3 = 0.761\ 904\ 7$$

The decimal for $\frac{16}{21}$ is $0.761\ 904\ 761\ 904$ ... which when rounded to the seventh decimal place differs from the calculator result. This discrepancy does not usually matter in practical questions.

Multiplying and dividing fractions

Earlier in the chapter, division was used to explain fractions: $\frac{3}{5}$ was the number produced from the division $3 \div 5$. In many textbooks fractions are explained by taking a cake, or pizza, or bar of chocolate (fractions often seem to involve food!) and dividing it into 5 or some other number of equal parts. The parts are then given out to various people. So one person might get $\frac{3}{5}$ while another gets $\frac{2}{5}$.

Fractions are explained as fractions of something. Although the whole something is often given as a single cake or pizza, this can be very confusing. Fractions are often fractions of several objects ('There were 40 people in the room; three-quarters of them were women') or fractions of something smaller than 1 ('As there are three of you, I'll split this remaining piece of pie into thirds'). In these cases 'pizza' diagrams can be less than helpful.

In dealing with multiplication and division of fractions you may have wondered about issues like these.

▶ Why does 'of' mean 'multiply' with fractions?

▶ Why must fractions be of the same kind to add and subtract, but not to multiply or divide?

▶ Why is divide 'turn upside-down and multiply' with fractions?

▶ Can multiplication of fractions be seen as 'repeated addition' as with whole numbers?

Part of the reason many people have problems is because the meaning of fractions changes. Fractions are first of all operators. So, three-sevenths operates on quantities: you can split the quantity into sevenths and then take three of the parts. This can be seen as taking three copies of one seventh of something. It is then not too difficult a step to consider what happens when you take three-sevenths of three-fifths of something.

If you look back to the introduction to rational numbers, you will see that a fraction becomes a label for a point, and then a number. This move to regarding three-sevenths as a number, divorced from any context of calculating three-sevenths of something, is subtle and sophisticated.

The use of words such as 'three-sevenths' rather than symbols is deliberate here. It is to help you think about the meaning of the fractions.

Rather than simply repeating methods for multiplying fractions that you have probably met many times before, the following tasks are designed to help you think about the nature of multiplying fractions.

Above, you were asked to consider three-sevenths as three copies of one-seventh. The following ask you to express other quantities as 'copies of'.

(a) What are one-half of two-sevenths, and one-third of three-sevenths in terms of 'copies of'?

(b) By thinking in terms of 'copies of', express the following in terms of parts of a whole:

  (i)   one-third of one-fifth of a whole, two-thirds of one-fifth of a whole;

  (ii) one-quarter of one-seventh of a whole, two-quarters of one-seventh of a whole;

  (iii) one-third of two-fifths of a whole, two-thirds of two-fifths of a whole.

(c) Make up more problems as in part (b). Write your questions and answers in fraction notation.

Comment

This activity is posed using words in order to emphasise the operator role of the number-names. It is useful when looking for patterns to use ordinary number-names. Notice that there is a sense of dividing up a whole into parts, and there is a number pattern to do with tops and bottoms which provide an equivalent 'single' operation.

Division of fractions can be thought of in a similar sense. Remember a statement such as 7 ÷ 2 means 'How many twos are there in seven?'.

| Task 27 | Dividing fractions |

Answer the following questions, paying attention to the patterns of numbers in each case. The following questions are indicators of a string of questions which can be used to draw attention to the fact that division of fractions is embedded in the language of fractions and of division.

▶ How many halves are in one? In two? In three? In ... ?

▶ How many thirds are in one? In two? In three? In ... ?

▶ How many quarters are in ... ?

▶ ... ?

What is the general pattern? (It should have emerged before you got to this point!)

Answer the next set of questions similarly.

▶ How many one-thirds are in one? How many two-thirds are in two? In three? ...

How many two-thirds are in two? In two twos? In two threes? ...In two thumps? In two bananas? In blob? In seven? In eight? In nine?

How many two-fifths are in two? In two twos? In two threes? ...In two thumps? In two bananas? In blob? In seven? In eight? In nine? ...

How many three-fifths are in three? In three twos? In three threes? ... In three thumps? In three bananas? In blob? In seven? In eight? In nine? ...

Comment

The intention here is that you start to recognise the pattern in the language and, by being able to say it in 'silly' examples you can think what the answer must be with other numbers. After becoming fluent in carrying out these tasks, it will help to write them down in fraction notation.

Multiplying decimals

When you have to multiply decimals without a calculator, you probably have some rules that you turn to. Two examples of these rules are:

when multiplying by 10 or 100, move the decimal point one or two places to the right;

when multiplying, e.g. 2.42 by 1.8, you work out how many decimal places there are in the answer by adding those in the two numbers.

Many people have such rules which they learned when they were taught how to carry out the calculations. There are various versions of these rules (do you move the decimal point or move the digits, do you line up the decimal points when multiplying or not?) which can lead to uncertainty. This section examines some of these difficulties.

Multiplying and dividing by powers of 10

Consider the multiplication $34.712 \times 100 = 3471.2$. What is happening with the 'move the decimal point' rule? It is easiest to see by laying out the numbers to show the values of each place:

	Thousands	Hundreds	Tens	Units		tenths	hundredths	thousandths
			3	4	.	7	1	2
× 100								
	3	4	7	1	.	2		

The decimal point does not actually move anywhere, it is the digits that move. To multiply by 10, the digits move one place to the left; to multiply by 100, the digits move two places to the left, and so on. Similarly, to divide by 10, the digits move one place to the right; to divide by 100, the digits move two places to the right, etc.

This is rather like talking about 'the sun rising in the morning'. It is the earth that is rotating, rather than the sun moving.

However, most of us imagine the decimal point moving. It is important to remember that imagining the decimal point moving is a quick method rather than an explanation of how, or why, the method works.

The rule for decimal places

Many people try to remember a rule for how many decimal places there will be after multiplying decimals. It is more reliable to work out an estimate of the answer rather than trying to remember a rule.

Consider the calculation 3.6 × 2.4. An approximation is:

3.6 ≈ 4 and 2.4 ≈ 2. Because 4 × 2 = 8, then 3.6 × 2.4 ≈ 8.

The actual answer is 8.64 which is approximately equal to 8. The approximation means that you can work out the magnitude of the answer. That is, you can find out if it is going to be about 8 or 80 or 0.8.

Task 28	Estimate and calculate

Use a calculator to find the following:

(a) 12.6 × 7.9

(b) 100.3 × 22.67

Comment

When using a calculator, it is very easy to type in the wrong number or for the calculator to give a false result if the batteries are low. Finding an approximation first means that you will know if your answer is of the correct magnitude. You need to know if the answer you are getting is reasonable.

Task 29	Going down

Now try this question:

52.3 × 0.4

Comment

Some students are surprised at the answer. This is usually because they believe that multiplying always gives a larger answer and dividing a smaller one. With fractions and decimals this is not always the case. Try multiplying other numbers by 0.4. Do they also decrease?

Explore with your calculator to find the range of numbers which decrease other numbers when multiplying.

Calculating with percentages

Percentages can be calculated using either fractions or decimals, although with a calculator, decimals are usually easier. You can also use the $\boxed{\%}$ on your calculator. How the $\boxed{\%}$ key works depends on the calculator type; you will need to experiment or consult your manual if you choose to use it.

Finding a percentage of something is straightforward provided you recall what the percentage notation means.

Percentage	Task 30

A building society offers 95% mortgages to first-time buyers. How much would the Smiths get on a house valued at £125 750?

Comment

$95\% = \frac{95}{100} = 0.95$

So 95% of £125 750 = 0.95 × £125 750 = £119 462.50

Two issues often cause difficulty with percentages:

▶ finding percentage increases or decreases;

▶ finding successive percentages, for example calculating VAT and service charge on a bill – does the order of calculating matter?

Many people work out a problem such as:

Find what £322 is after a 15% increase

by carrying out a two-stage calculation, first finding 15%, and then adding it on. This method works, of course, but you can use your awareness of the connections between percentages and decimals to simplify the calculation. Finding a percentage increase of 15% is the same as finding 115% of the original. This percentage can be written as a decimal, 1.15, and then calculated in the same way as any other percentage. So:

£322 increased by 15% = 1.15 × £322 = £370.30

The same applies to decreases: a 10% discount will give 90% of the original, so multiply by 0.9.

On many bills, for example in restaurants, VAT is added at 17.5% and sometimes also a service charge of 15%. Does it make any difference to what you have to pay if the VAT is added first then the service charge, or vice versa?

Make up some examples to try. Remember to keep them simple. The examples are special cases; from these examples you are trying to work out what will always happen – the general case.

Comment

Take a restaurant bill of £16.

Adding VAT first means calculating (100% + 17.5%) of £16:

  117.5% of £16 = 1.175 × £16 = £18.80

Adding the service charge on top is (100% + 15%) of £18.80:

  115% of £18.80 = 1.15 × £18.80 = £21.62

Adding the extras the other way round:

  115% of £16 = 1.15 × £16 = £18.40
  117.5 % of £18.40 = 1.175 × £18.40 = £21.62

This is the same total amount. Can you see why this is so?

Looking at the general case can sometimes make a result clearer. Suppose the amount of the bill is, say, £n.

Adding the VAT first gives:

  117.5% of £n = 1.175 × £n

Adding the service charge now gives:

  115% of (1.175 × £n) = 1.15 × 1.175 × £n

This is an example of the commutative property of multiplication. See Chapter 5.

At this point you may be able to see that the order does not matter. Multiplying by the two decimals 1.15 and 1.175 can take place in any order.

Summary

This chapter has looked at working with numbers using different approaches to the usual text book ones.

It has covered:

▶ types of numbers and how they are represented;

▶ aspects and issues of mental, calculator and written methods;

▶ working with fractions, decimals and percentages.

Further study

Holmes, H. and Allen, B. (2006) *Starting with Maths*, The Open University. *Starting with Maths* is a course designed to help you feel more confident in using mathematics in a variety of different situations – at home, in work or in your other studies.

Graham, L. and Sargent, D. (1981) *Countdown to Mathematics*, vol. 1, Prentice Hall. *Countdown to Mathematics*, volume 1, includes a module on basic skills and techniques in arithmetic and includes diagnostic questions, plenty of examples to try yourself, and full solutions.

Graham, A.T. (2003) *Basic Mathematics*, Teach Yourself. *Basic Mathematics* is aimed at teaching you all the maths you need to know for everyday living.

3 Measures and proportion

Introduction

This chapter is concerned with measures and their uses. The issues considered include the following:

◗ the purpose of measurement;

◗ absolute and relative comparison;

◗ discrete and continuous measures;

◗ use of units;

◗ gradients and trigonometric ratios.

The chapter is subdivided into four parts:

◗ measurement and comparison;

◗ measurement scales;

◗ other measurement issues;

◗ ratio and proportion.

Measurement and comparison

Measurements are made in particular contexts and for particular purposes.

Task 32	Measurements

(a) Think about recent situations where you have measured something. Consider issues such as why, what, and how you measured as well as the units and instruments you used and the accuracy you needed.

(b) Now think about other situations where things are compared. Consider how the comparison is expressed and what is important in making a comparison.

Comment

The context and purpose of a measurement determines the appropriate tools and units to use and the quality of the measurement required.

(a) Measurements can be made in order to describe or distinguish between two or more objects, but are more usually undertaken for comparison – either of two or more objects or an object and a given measurement. For example, suppose you wished to fit a piece of furniture into a fixed space. If the furniture is already in your possession then a piece of string will be sufficient to compare the space and the object to assess fit, taking care to establish the boundaries (minimum space and maximum object width). However, if the furniture is to be purchased from a catalogue then the space measurement may be more critical and a steel measuring tape may be a more appropriate tool to measure the space in millimetres (or whatever units are used in the catalogue).

(b) There is a vast variety of situations where things are compared qualitatively or quantitatively; it is part of making sense of the world. Comparisons can be made informally (brighter, warmer, larger), by category (large, medium, small) or some quantitative measure such as a physical measure or a statistical measure, e.g. birth rate. An overriding consideration is that a comparison should in some sense be fair – that 'like is compared to like'.

There are two ways of making comparisons between two numerical quantities. One is the 'difference'. This is based on subtracting the lesser amount from the other and is called an 'absolute' comparison. However, in many circumstances such direct comparison may not be useful, informative, or even fair; and a different measure of the relationship, such as a ratio makes more sense. Such comparisons are 'relative'.

Absolute or relative	Task 33

Which kind of comparison would you use to get useful or fair information for the following?

(a) The ages of two children.

(b) Prices.

(c) Population changes in different countries.

(d) Pay rises.

Comment

Absolute comparison is usually used when comparing a few similar items; for example, Harry is 3 years older than Alice, or this car costs £1000 more than that. Relative comparisons can be more useful when looking at changes over time and over a range of items; for example, changes in the general price of food compared to electronic items over the last 10 years. When comparing dissimilar items or ones with unequal bases *absolute* figures are generally useless by themselves. A *relative* measure such as proportion or percentage will ensure that the comparison is fairer; for example, in making comparisons between countries of different size and in comparing pay rises.

However, there are no hard and fast rules.

Pay rises are usually stated as relative, say 3%, rather than absolute (so many £ per year). This may seem fair, but for a low paid worker on say £5.35/hr a

3% rise is equivalent to an increase of £334/year, whereas for an executive on £100,000/year it is an increase of £3000.

Sometimes both types of difference are relevant; for example, when travelling, you may want to know how much further you have to go (absolute), but you may also be interested in the distance relative to the whole journey.

Errors in measurements are usually calculated as relative errors, because an error of 1 m in a journey of a 1000 km is rather different to an error of 1 m when measuring something small like the size of a room, or a sofa!

There are a number of techniques for making comparisons more useful and fairer, particularly when dealing with large or differing populations and when uncertainties are involved. These are the realm of statistical measures and some of these are considered in Chapter 4.

This chapter is concerned with the nature of physical measures and uses of the relative measures of proportion and ratio.

Measurement scales

Both names (categories) and numbers are frequently used in measures, and are seen on graphs. It is important to differentiate when numbers are being used as labels and when as a numerical measure of some kind since this determines which, if any, calculations can be made and what inferences can be deduced from graphs.

Task 34	Labels and measures

Look around your home and area and make a note of any numbers you see and try to categorise them. Think about what the numbers indicate in each case.

Comment

For example, a house number is a label, whereas 11.10 on the digital clock indicates the time of day, 2 loaves of bread on a shopping list, 88–92 FM as a radio frequency all use numbers as magnitudes.

One useful way of understanding the differing uses of numbers as measures is the Stevens taxonomy (Stevens, 1946).

Naming scales

▶ **Nominal** (or naming). Naming scales are simply names or labels that might be used as categories for counting purposes. These are most commonly words, for example names or colours; but can be numbers. These are not quantitative so have no natural ordering and no arithmetic properties. Examples of nominal numbers include pin numbers, race numbers and bus routes.

▶ **Ordinal** (or ordered). Examples are days of the week or positions in a race (first, second, etc.). An order is sometimes only implied (for example, excellent, good, satisfactory, unsatisfactory, poor), and although numbers can be used to describe an ordering scale, there is no zero-point, and no meaningful interval between positions. A runner in a race who comes in fourth has done better than one who comes in sixth, but knowing that a runner finishes two places behind a rival in a race does not provide any information about the how far apart they were, nor anything about the runners in between.

Numerical scales

▶ **Interval**. Here numbers are also used to indicate the relative positioning. However, interval scales are numerical; there is an ordering (3 o'clock follows 2 o'clock) and the intervals between points on the scale have meaning – for example, 2:30 is half way between 2 and 3 o'clock. Unlike ordinal scales there can be a zero but it is an arbitrary point rather than a zero quantity; for example the zero of the 24-hour clock does not imply 'no time', just as 0 °C does not mean 'no heat'. Interval scales have some numerical qualities – they can be added to or subtracted for absolute comparison, 6 o'clock is 4 hours later than 2 o'clock; but ratios, relative comparisons, have no meaning: 6 o'clock is not three times as late as 2 o'clock!

▶ **Ratio**. Here numbers indicate magnitude. Examples are most measurements such as length, weight, elapsed time (as opposed to clock time). Unlike interval scales, these have the full range of properties of numbers. Zero really does mean a zero quantity and the order of points, the interval between points and ratios are meaningful. So a length of 0 cm really means no length, the interval between 2 cm and 3 cm is the same as between 3 cm and 4 cm, 2.5 cm has meaning, and a length of 10 cm is twice as much as a length of 5 cm. Both absolute and relative comparisons can be calculated.

Some numerical scales are restricted to take a particular set of values (for example, numbers of people have to be whole numbers), whereas other scales, such as length, weight or time elapsed permit magnitudes corresponding to any number at all.

Discrete and continuous scales

A discrete measure is one that can only take particular values with gaps in between, for example, a count can only be a whole number, off-the-peg clothes come in particular sizes (which could include half-sizes). A continuous measure is one where any number can be a possible value, for example, a body measurement, theoretically at least you can be 1.69 m or 1.6902634256 m.

Think about clothing sizes and what fits you. How are off-the-peg clothes marked? What if you could afford to have something made for you ...?

Comment

Off-the-peg sizes are discrete – they may be labelled S, M, L, XL, or with numbers 10, 12, 14 ..., or measurements as in collar sizes 16, $16\frac{1}{2}$, 17, $17\frac{1}{2}$.

The sizes are presumably imposed upon a continuous spectrum – but how often have you felt that, for example, M is too small but L is too large ...?

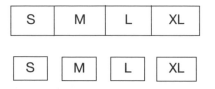

When a measure is expressed in different units the relationships between numbers is exact: 2170 mm is identical to 217 cm, even though measurement is always approximate. It is not possible to say that the width of a room measures exactly 2170 mm. This is due to the nature of measurement involving continuous scales: there can never be perfect precision. The best you can do is to get an approximate measurement. Precision is used to describe the degree to which a measurement is reproducible indicated by how many decimal places the measurement claims to represent, while accuracy is used to describe the error bounds within which the assumed 'true measurement' lies.

One way of clarifying the terms precision and accuracy is to imagine target shooting:

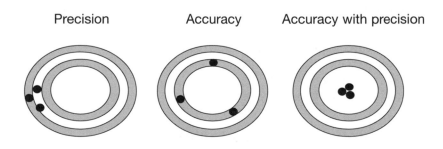

Sources of inaccuracy include:

◗   human error in, for example, lining up the measuring mark exactly opposite the object being measured (boundary definition);

◗   quality of measurement tool used (precision available);

◗   conditions under which the measurement is made (for example, temperature and/or pressure).

Showing the accuracy of a measurement

In everyday tasks such as cooking or DIY (do it yourself) the small errors that creep into measuring can be offset by a person's skill. In work situations such as a hospital, pharmacy or in manufacturing, knowing the size of possible measurement errors is crucial, so they need to be both quantified and stated. There are several ways of doing this. As an example, take a measurement such as 5 g of a substance weighed on digital scales which read to the nearest gram. This means that the mass could be as low as 4.5 g which is called the lower bound (or limit) or it could be almost (but not quite) 5.5 g at the upper bound (or limit).

The usual practice for rounding a value is that if it ends in 5 (e.g. 3.5 or 7.5) it rounds up. So here 4.5 would round up to 5 and 5.5 would round up to 6.

This range of possible values can be expressed in several different ways:

5 g to nearest gram;

5 ± 0.5 g (in the form $m \pm e$, e is called the error bound);

a value m, where $4.5 \le m < 5.5$.

or in a picture:

(In this diagram, the filled-in circle shows that the lowest value is included; the open circle shows that 5.5 is not included.)

Error bound Task 36

Using the convention $m \pm e$ quoted above, express, the range of possible values for:

(a) 25 minutes measured to the nearest minute;

(b) 400 ml measured to the nearest 5 ml;

(c) 180 °C measured to the nearest 10 °C;

(d) 20 cm measured to the nearest 0.2 cm.

Comment

(a) $25 \pm \frac{1}{2}$ minute (or $\pm$ 0.5 minute or $\pm$ 30 s)

(b) 400 ± 2.5 ml

(c) 180 ± 5 °C

(d) 20 ± 0.1 cm

This way of stating errors uses the actual value of the error and is called the absolute error. For example, suppose sugar is weighed on scales which read to the nearest 5 grams. With this particular set of scales every reading will have the same absolute error, which is ± 2.5 grams. But this amount of error will have a relatively greater effect on a small reading than on a large one. Percentages can be used to express this relative error.

For an item weighing 25 grams:

$\frac{2.5}{25} \times 100 = 10\%$ So the relative error is 25 grams ± 10%.

For an item weighing 250 grams:

$\frac{2.5}{25} \times 100 = 1\%$ So the relative error is 250 grams ± 1%.

Using measurements in calculations

It is important to appreciate that any errors made in measuring affect any subsequent calculation. For example, if the length of an item is measured and the reading is recorded as 645 mm, this implies an accuracy of 645 mm to the nearest millimetre so the error lies within ± 0.5 mm. If you had reason to multiply the length by 10, then the error is repeated 10 times, so the error becomes: ± 0.5 × 10 = ±5 mm.

It is recognised that measurements of manufactured items cannot be completely accurate so the measurement of error is called tolerance, an allowable variation. Tolerances of resistors used in electronics are quoted in percentages so a resistor with a tolerance of 5% is of better quality than one with a tolerance of 10%.

The aspect of tolerance or error is so important that it is a very reasonable stance to take that any number which is claimed to be a measurement *must* be accompanied by the error or tolerance. Thus 34.5 cm is not a measurement, whereas 34.5 ± 0.2 cm is. Usually, as indicated above, the error is taken to be ±5 in the next 'decimal' place unless stated otherwise.

Other measurement issues

The importance of standard measurements becomes evident when you want to communicate a measurement to another person. You could go into a DIY store with a piece of string to measure the length of the window blind that you need. But if you needed to order a blind then including the piece of string with the order form would not be acceptable, a standard measure would be needed.

Units of measurement

In the UK there are three systems of units of measurement in use: imperial, metric and SI (Système Internationale).

The foot, pound, second system

The foot, pound, second system (fps) is often referred to as the imperial system. When imperial measures were first used they were based on the sort of amounts that people commonly used, or on parts of the human body. This means that the relationships between units are unplanned and seem very arbitrary.

12 inches = 1 foot

3 feet = 1 yard

1760 yards = 1 mile

16 ounces = 1 pound

14 pounds = 1 stone

2240 pounds = 1 ton

Converting between units is thus quite complicated. For example:

2180 inches = 181 feet 8 inches = 60 yards 1 foot 8 inches

Notice also that decimals are rarely used with imperial measures (2180 inches would be 181.6666667 feet).

The introduction of metrication means that imperial units are gradually going out of use in the UK though, currently, miles continue to be used for road signs and related measurements of speed and distance.

The metric system

By contrast to the imperial system, the metric system was designed as a whole with the relationships between units following a logical pattern by being based on multiples of ten.

For example, the distance cycled in a day is likely to be given in kilometres (abbreviated to km), a person's height in metres (m) and their waist measurement in centimetres (cm). The prefixes 'kilo' and 'centi', together with 'milli', are used throughout the metric system. Here they are illustrated with measures of length:

It was introduced by Napoleon as part of his rationalisation of thought and action at all levels of French society and practices.

'kilo' means 1000, so a kilometre (km) is 1000 metres;

'centi' means $\frac{1}{100}$, so a centimetre (cm) is $\frac{1}{100}$ metre or 0.01 m;

(there are 100 centimetres in a metre);

'milli' means $\frac{1}{1000}$, so a millimetre (mm) is $\frac{1}{1000}$ metre or 0.001 m;

(there are 1000 millimetres in a metre).

There are other prefixes, much less commonly used – 'deci', 'deca', 'hecto':

1 decametre = 10 metres ('deca' means 10);

1 hectometre = 100 metres ('hecto' means 100);

1 decimetre = $\frac{1}{10}$ metre or 0.1 m ('deci' means 1/10).

Of course these metric prefixes ('kilo', etc.) are used for other units besides those of length: kilograms (kg), millilitres (ml) and so on. These

It is easy to confuse the worlds 'decimetre' and 'decametre' (which is possibly the reason they are seldom used).

Sometimes thousands are separated by commas e.g. 10,000; however, using a space prevents confusion with the continental system of using a comma to separate whole and decimal parts (the UK uses the decimal point).

simple relationships mean that it is easy to convert measurements in, say, centimetres or metres; for example, 2170 mm = 217 cm = 2.17 m.

Système Internationale (SI) system

The SI system is a version of the metric system used in science and engineering. Its aim was to simplify and standardise the prefixes ('kilo' etc.) and so to avoid mistakes due to misplaced decimal points. For example, the base unit of length in the SI system is the metre and all other units are related to it in multiples of 1000. There are 1000 metres in 1 kilometre (km) and 1 millimetre (mm) is one-thousandth of a metre. The prefixes used in the SI system are standard for any quantity within it, so if you know the base units you can work out the naming and the values of the rest. Here are some of the prefixes used.

Prefix	Symbol	Figures	Words	Powers of 10
Giga	G	1 000 000 000	A thousand millions (a billion)	10^9
Mega	M	1 000 000	A million	10^6
Kilo	k	1 000	A thousand one	10^3
		1	One	10^0
Milli	m	0.001	A thousandth	10^{-3}
Micro	μ	0.000 001	A millionth	10^{-6}
Nano	n	0.000 000 001	A thousand millionth	10^{-9}

μ, the symbol used for 'micro', is the Greek letter pronounced 'mu'.

In the world of computing, 'mega' and 'giga' are often used; confusingly a gigabyte can be used to mean 1 000 000 000 bytes (e.g. for size of hard disk) or 1 073 741 824 bytes, equal to 2^{30} bytes (e.g. for memory size).

Notice that centimetres, for example, are not used in the SI system, because a centimetre is $\frac{1}{100}$ metre and $\frac{1}{100}$ ths of a unit are not used.

Aspects of area, volume and angle are discussed in Chapter 6.

Other measures

Some other things you might measure are perimeter, area, volume, capacity, time, temperature, mass and angles.

Perimeter and area

Perimeter is the distance around a plane (2D) shape, whereas area is the amount of space within. In the SI system area is measured in square metres (m2).

Land is measured in hectares equal to 10 000 m^2, which is about 2.47 acres in the imperial system.

What is the difference between a park which is 50 km square and one of 50 km²?

Comment

The first is taken to mean that it is a square, 50 km on each side, so with a perimeter of 200 km and an area of 2500 km². The second gives a measure of space, an area, but with no indication of shape so there is no information on the perimeter either.

Volume or capacity

Volume and capacity are sometimes distinguished, with volume being how much space a 3D object displaces measured in cubic measure, e.g. metres (m3), whereas capacity is often used for how much a container can hold. Capacity uses fluid measure, e.g. litres (a litre is 1000 cm³), cups, fluid ounces.

Angle

Angle is an amount of turn and is often measured in everyday life in terms of complete turns or quarter turns (right angles). An angle is formed by two lines sharing a common endpoint, the vertex.

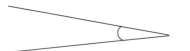

The units commonly used are degrees (symbol °) with there being 360° in a complete turn. The degree is further subdivided into 60 minutes (') each of 60 seconds ("), which is a direct legacy from Babylonian astronomers of around 2500 BCE. Engineers sometimes use gradians (abbreviated to grads where 400 grads = 1 full revolution) while mathematicians use radians (2π radians = 1 full revolution).

Angles in degrees are used to define location on the earth's surface using latitude (angle North or South from the equator) and longitude (angle East or West of the prime meridian). One minute of latitude is one nautical mile, and officially taken to be 1852 metres; a knot being a speed of one nautical mile per hour.

Scientific calculators commonly have two modes for working with angles – degrees and radians – and it is important to set the mode correctly depending on the angular measure being used.

The radian is the SI measure for angle; defined as the angle subtended at the centre of a circle by an arc of the circumference equal in length to the radius of the circle.

π is the ratio of the circumference to the diameter for any circle.

There are 2000 × π milliradians in a circle. So a milliradian is just over 1/6283 of a circle. Range finding equipment use approximations of this, e.g. NATO defines a 'mil' as $\frac{1}{64\,000}$ of a circle which is easier to divide into many parts.

Time

The SI base unit for time is the second (s). Small amounts of time will be measured in milliseconds (ms) or even microseconds (µs) or nanoseconds.

Temperature

The common unit of temperature is degrees Celsius (°C), although many people still use the Fahrenheit system (°F), especially for hot weather ('It was in the nineties'). Both Celsius and Fahrenheit are interval scales – there is an arbitrary zero (for example 0 °C is the freezing point of water at normal pressure). The SI unit of temperature is the Kelvin (°K) but this unit is mainly used in science, where 0 °K means that there is no heat energy present at all (no movement of fundamental particles … and in fact is unobtainable!). Thus Kelvin is a ratio scale not just an interval scale.

Mass and weight

The terms 'mass' and 'weight' can cause confusion. Mass is the amount of matter in an object and does not alter wherever you are in the universe. For most everyday purposes, the mass and weight of an object are treated as the same because the gravitational force does not vary much on Earth. If an object was moved to the Moon, although its mass would remain the same, its weight would decrease because gravity on the Moon is less than on Earth.

The SI unit of mass is the gram. Weight is a measure of force and depends on the force of gravity on the object. In the SI system it is measured in newtons (N) where a newton is the amount of force required to accelerate a mass of one kilogram by 1 metre per second squared (1 N = 1 kg × m/s^2).

Conversion from one system of units to another

Even with a single system of units it can be confusing to convert one unit to another, especially in units such as those for area.

Task 38	Square units

The area of a shape is 1.5 m^2. What is this in cm^2? (It might help to draw a quick sketch.)

Comment

It is tempting to say that because there are 100 centimetres in 1 metre:

$$1.5 \text{ m}^2 = 1.5 \times 100 = 150 \text{ cm}^2$$

This is not the correct answer. If you need convincing, draw a square and mark the sides 1 m = 100 cm. The area of the square is:

$$1 \text{ m} \times 1 \text{ m} = 1 \text{ m}^2 \text{ or } 100 \text{ cm} \times 100 \text{ cm} = 10\ 000 \text{ cm}^2$$

So an area of 1.5 m² equals $1.5 \times 10\ 000 = 15\ 000 \text{ cm}^2$.

Because both metric and imperial units are used in the UK, people frequently have problems when measures are expressed in a system different to the one they find familiar. Most people find that they are confident with only one system of units for any particular purpose. This may be metric for some measures and imperial for others. They may, for example, feel happy measuring kitchen cabinets in millimetres or buying petrol in litres, but read their car speed in miles per hour. Where there is a need in everyday use to convert from one system to another, most people use easy reference points such as:

30 cm is about the same length as 1 foot;

1 metre is slightly longer than a yard;

1 kilogram is slightly more than 2lb;

5 miles is about the same as 8 kilometres.

These are often good enough for everyday purposes.

For more exact conversions you need to use a calculation method using a conversion (or scale) factor. If you have several conversions to make, it may be quicker to use the constant facility on your calculator. If you wanted to refer to the results later you could produce a conversion graph or a conversion table.

Many people refer to a 1 kg bag of sugar as 'a 2-pound bag' or say 'half-a-pound of butter' when they refer to a 250 g packet.

You may find that, like many people, you get confused about which way round to do a conversion calculation using a scale factor. For example, if you are told that:

4.55 litres = 1 gallon.

This is example of ratio as a scaling.

What scale factor do you multiply 6 gallons by to change into litres? And to change 35 litres into gallons? A diagram can help:

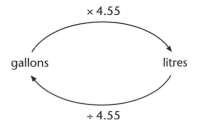

Gallons and litres are used as conversion examples for the rest of this section.

A US gallon is less than a UK one (the former is 3.79 litres).

Converting one way is 'doing', in this case multiplying by 4.55. Converting the other way is 'undoing'; here, dividing by 4.55.

Calculator constant and conversion table

If you have to carry out a series of conversion calculations of the same kind (for example currency conversion), a good method is to use the constant facility on your calculator. This could be used to draw up a conversion table. You will see such tables for litres and gallons on petrol pumps; one converting gallons to litres is shown below.

Gallons	Litres
0	0
1	4.55
2	9.10
3	13.65
4	18.20
5	22.75
6	27.30
7	31.85
8	36.40
9	40.95
10	45.50

A disadvantage of the table is that conversions from whole numbers of litres to gallons are not easy to do.

Task 39	Converting back

Create a table for converting litres to gallons using the constant facility on your calculator. A suitable range would be every 5 litres from 0 to 50.

Graphical method

Setting up a conversion graph takes time, but once it is done the graph provides a quick visual method of converting units in both directions. It involves mapping one set of measurements onto another. The drawback is that the accuracy is limited by the scale used.

Drawing a conversion graph — Task 40

Once again work with a range of 0 to 10 gallons. The technique for all conversion graphs that involve a constant scale factor (4.55 in this case) is to produce a straight line joining two known conversion values. Two known values here are:

0 gallons = 0 litres;
1 gallon = 4.55 litres.

These would be close together on most graphs, so for more accuracy a better second pair of values would be:

10 gallons = 45.5 litres

On a piece of graph paper, draw in two axes as in the diagram in Task 41 and label the horizontal axis (or x-axis) 'gallons' and the vertical axis (or y-axis) 'litres'. Mark in an equally spaced scale for gallons (0–10) and one for litres (0–50).

Plot the two points (0,0) and (10, 45.5) and join up the points to make a straight line.

Using the graph — Task 41

Suppose you bought 35 litres of petrol at the garage and wanted to know how many gallons that is. Use the graph to find out.

Comment

Drawing a horizontal line from the 35 litre mark on the vertical axis to meet the graph line and then drawing a line vertically down to meet the x-axis you can read off that 35 litres is about 7.7 gallons.

This does not give as precise an answer as the calculation method.

When using the information from both methods you can see that:

number of litres = 4.55 × number of gallons

If the number of litres is called y and the equivalent number of gallons x then

$$y = 4.55x$$

All graphs involving a constant scale factor are of this form, $y = kx$ where k is a fixed number. In the case of changing gallons to litres, $k = 4.55$.

Note the algebraic convention that $4.55x$ means 4.55 multiplied by x.

If you reflect the graph in the line $y = x$, then you get the graph for the undoing, converting litres to gallons by dividing by 4.55

Graphs of this kind are discussed in Algebra, pages 117–18.

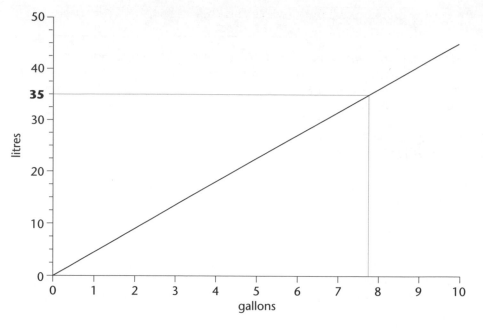

If you have access to a graphing calculator or a computer spreadsheet application, you can produce both a graph that gives x and y values, and a conversion table.

Task 42	Using technology

For a graphics calculator

Put in the function $y = 4.55\,x$, set the WINDOW to the same setting as in the graphing task above and draw the graph. This should be a straight line passing through the origin (0,0). Use the TRACE key to move the cursor along the line. The coordinates of the cursor will be displayed. In this case the x values are the number of gallons and the y values are the number of litres. If your calculator has a TABLE facility, this can now be used to show equivalent amounts for gallons and litres.

For a spreadsheet application

Set up a two-column table as shown below (once the formulas in A4 and B3 have been entered they can be copied down).

	A	B
		fx =4.55*A3
1		
2	gallons	litres
3	1	=4.55*A3
4	=A3+0.5	=4.55*A4
5	=A4+0.5	=4.55*A5
6	=A5+0.5	=4.55*A6

To get the graph, highlight the table and choose an XY (scatter) chart.

Comment

Gallons	Litres to 1 decimal place
1	4.6
1.5	6.8
2	9.1
2.5	11.4
3	13.7
3.5	15.9
4	18.2
4.5	20.5
5	22.8
5.5	25.0
6	27.3
6.5	29.6
7	31.9
7.5	34.1
8	36.4
8.5	38.7
9	41.0
9.5	43.2
10	45.5

A plotting program could also be used to obtain the graph by plotting $y = 4.55x$.

Links between quantities: rates and compound units

The units discussed so far have been for single quantities, but quantities expressed as rates (for example, speeds) require compound units.

Speeds of vehicles such as cars, bicycles or trains are usually given as miles per hour or kilometres per hour. A sprinter's speed may be quoted in metres per second; a child's growth in centimetres per year. Each of these units are given as unit of length per unit of time.

Other examples of rates are:

▶ density, measured in kilograms per cubic metre (kg/cm^3);

▶ rate of flow, measured in litres per second (l/s);

▶ fuel consumption, measured in miles per gallon (mpg);

pressure in lb per cubic inch or kg per cc (and then re-labelled as millibars, e.g. barometric pressure or tyre pressure).

It is usual in imperial units to abbreviate miles per hour as mph, or miles per gallon as mpg. In the metric and SI systems 'p' is not used as an abbreviation for 'per'. Instead, metres per second is written m/s or ms^{-1}.

With rates you have to interpret the numbers with more care than when using simple units. One of the difficulties of rates is that they can be read in two ways. For example, the population density of a region might be 807 people/km^2. This means that there are on average 807 people for each square kilometre, or if everyone was distributed uniformly, then there would be 807 people in each square kilometre.

But this figure might be given the other way round. How much space does each person have? In this case the figure would be found by reversing (undoing) the scaling.

$$1 \text{ km}^2 \xrightarrow{\times 807} 807 \text{ people}$$

$$1 \div 807 \xleftarrow{\div 807} 1 \text{ person}$$
$$= 0.00124 \text{ km}^2$$

That is, one person has:

$$1 \div 807 = 0.001\ 24 \text{ km}^2$$

This small value is not easy to interpret, so it might be preferable in m^2. This converts as:

$$1000 \times 1000 \times 0.001\ 24 \text{ m}^2 = 1240 \text{ m}^2$$

which is the amount of space per person.

Task 43	Comparing fuel consumptions

Consider the situation when a new model of a car is brought out. If the fuel consumption of the new model is 30 mpg as against the 25 mpg of the old one, what does this tell you?

Comment

You will probably say that 30 mpg is better than 25 mpg as the car travels more miles for the same amount of petrol (one gallon). It is also possible to think about this the other way round. For a journey of 25 miles, the previous model of car used 1 gallon; the new one will not use as much (since it can go 30 miles for 1 gallon). Thus for a fixed length of journey you will use less petrol.

However, if you look at a current brochure for a new car you may be surprised by some of the figures given for fuel consumption. For example an extract from a Vauxhall Corsa Expression (2006) gives the fuel consumption of a 1.0i model as:

mpg (litres/100km)		
Urban driving	Extra-urban driving	Combined figure
40.9 (6.9)	64.2 (4.4)	53.3 (5.3)

As you might expect, the imperial values show that fuel consumption is better (in terms of getting more miles for each gallon of petrol for out-of-town driving). But how do you interpret the metric values? Instead of apparently increasing from urban driving to non-urban driving, they go down. Yet in each case the figures quoted are for the same model of the same car. In the second case, you may have noticed that the rate of consumption is the other way round, as the number of litres for each 100 kilometres of distance travelled. It gives how much fuel is used for a fixed distance.

Rates can be complicated to understand and interpret. As they are mainly used for comparison purposes (in the above case in order to make decisions about efficiency or value for money) it is important to know what the figures are telling you.

Checking the conversion	Task 44

Check whether the figures for the Corsa car given above are correct. Do you agree that urban consumption of 40.9 mpg is equivalent to 6.9 litres per 100 km?

There are three conversions to carry out:

▶ gallons to litres;

▶ miles to kilometres;

▶ kilometres per litre to litres per 100 kilometres.

You will need two conversion factors:

1 gallon = 4.55 litres;

1 mile = 1.609 km.

This task is quite exacting. If you can carry it out successfully, you have a good grasp of conversions.

Comment

Here is one possible solution. You may have reached the same answer but have done it in a different way or in a different order. That does not matter. The important thing is that you can follow your working and someone else seeing it for the first time could also follow it.

The rate of petrol consumption is given as 40.9 miles per gallon.

Changing gallons to litres. Since 4.55 litres is approximately equal to 1 gallon there will be fewer miles for one litre:

$40.9 \div 4.55 = 8.989$ miles per litre.

Changing miles to kilometres. 1 mile = 1.609 km approximately:

$8.989 \times 1.609 = 14.463$ km per litre.

But the table shows litres per kilometre and not vice versa. Taking the reciprocal:

If you wondered why 3 decimal places was suggested earlier it is this stage that it could make a difference.

14.463 km per litre $= \frac{1}{14.463}$ litre per km $= 0.069$ litre per km;

$0.069 \times 100 = 6.9$ litre per 100 km.

This is the value given in the table.

If you have access to a graphics calculator you can see the stages on the screen. Set your calculator to read 3 decimal places.

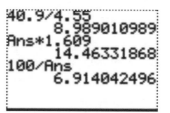

Conversion between units using a rate (as in 'rate of exchange') is a particular use of ratio.

Ratio and proportion

Ratio is a fundamental theme running throughout mathematics: it is one of the ways of comparing one thing relative to another and is used extensively in geometry, algebra and trigonometry. If you want to decide if two expressions or two values are equal, you can subtract them and check to see how close their difference is to zero, or you can take their ratio and see how close this is to 1.

The idea of ratio relates to situations where there are two (or more) quantities and you are interested in preserving the fraction that one is of the other (or the fraction that one is of their sum. For example, in the action of picking strawberries, the rule '2 for me and 3 for the pot, 2 for me and 3 for the pot ...' ensures that, however many I pick, I always eat two-fifths of them – the ratio of 2 to 5 is preserved. In geometry, examples of ratio apply to scaling a shape such as a rectangle, so that all the lengths are, say doubled, thus preserving the ratio of the lengths of the sides. Proportion is a statement that two ratios are equal. Thus the two rectangles shown are in the same proportion because the ratios of their adjacent edge lengths are equal. Put another way, a is to b as c is to d is a proportion; a is to b is a ratio.

The word 'analogy' comes from the Greek for proportion.

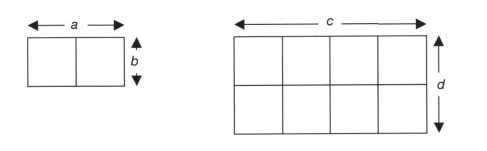

Jot down at least three examples of use for each of the words ratio and proportion.

Try to write notes on the similarities and differences.

Comment

The following are some examples.

Ratio: map scales (1:25 000), scale model (1:72), gear ratio (1 to 10.82), share price–earning ratio (P/E or PER) of 15, pupil–teacher ratio of 17.1, road gradients (1:5, 10%).

Proportion: 15% of the population is over 65 years of age, mix mortar in the proportions of 2 parts sand to 1 part cement.

Ratios are normally, but not always, written using the ':' symbol and simplified to the form of '1:a number'. Ratio of 6 to 4 is 6:4 or 6/4 and is the same as a ratio of 3:2 or 3/2. The notation 3/2 associates a value with a ratio. Whereas 6/4 and 3/2 are different as fractions, they have the same 'value' as ratios, hence the term rational numbers for the number system of arithmetic using their values.

The following sections illustrate the use of ratio in various mathematical topics.

A particular ratio, π

The ratio of the circumference of any circle to its diameter is always the same whatever the actual measurements. This ratio is denoted by the Greek letter pi π which is an irrational real number and has a constant value approximately equal to 3.141592 … .

The number of letters in each word of 'How I wish I could calculate pi' is one way of remembering the first few digits of π.

See Chapter 6.

If two shapes are mathematically similar and the same size they are said to be congruent. In other words, the scale factor is 1 and the ratio of corresponding sides has the value 1:1 or 1/1 also known as 1.

Similarity

The term 'similar' is very precise in mathematics. Unlike everyday language where the term might mean 'the same in many or most respects', in mathematics it means having exactly the same shape which implies having corresponding angles equal. Two similar figures are scaled versions of each other, and so corresponding sides are scaled by the same amount. The ratios of corresponding edges are the same, hence the figures are 'in proportion'

Task 46	Similar or not?

Which of the following pairs of shapes are similar in the mathematical sense? (It may help to draw diagrams.)

(a) Any 2 squares.

(b) Any two rectangles.

(c) Any two circles.

(d) Any two equilateral triangles (an equilateral triangle is one with all three sides equal in length and all three angles equal in size).

(e) Any two right-angled triangles.

Comment

(a) Yes.

(b) No; although rectangles have equal corresponding angles, any two rectangles may not have corresponding sides in proportion, e.g.

(c) Yes.

(d) Yes.

(e) No; the non 90° corresponding angles may not necessarily be equal.

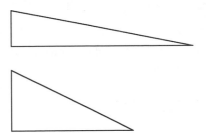

In general all sets of regular plane shapes are similar, e.g. regular pentagons, hexagons, octagons … semicircles …

Knowledge of some of the dimensions of similar figures enables other dimensions to be calculated.

Trigonometric ratios

If two right-angled triangles are similar, then the ratio of the lengths of any one pair of sides in one triangle is equal to the ratio of the lengths of the corresponding sides in the other triangle.

Remember not all right-angled triangles are similar.

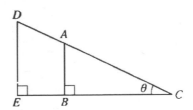

For example,

$$\frac{AB}{BC} = \frac{DE}{EC} \text{ and } \frac{BC}{CA} = \frac{EC}{CD}$$

This is known by many people as Thales' theorem. It states effectively that each angle has an invariant measure, whether it appears in a huge triangle or a tiny one: the ratio of corresponding pairs of sides is constant. This then gives a way to measure angles using ratios. Start with the right-angled triangle ABC. Then any of the three ratios $\frac{AB}{AC}$, $\frac{BC}{AC}$ or $\frac{AB}{BC}$ will capture the size of the angle θ uniquely as long as the angle is less than 90°.

Such ratios are called the trigonometric ratios and can be used for calculating lengths and angles in right-angled triangles. The three basic trigonometric ratios have particular names, sine, cosine and tangent, and are defined overleaf.

Greek letters are often used to indicate angles. θ is said 'theta'.

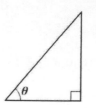

If θ is an acute angle in any right-angled triangle, then the sine of θ, abbreviated to sin θ, is defined as

The hypotenuse is the longest side – the one opposite the right-angle.

$$\sin \theta = \frac{\text{length of side opposite to } \theta}{\text{length of hypotenuse}}.$$

The cosine of θ, abbreviated to cos θ, is defined as

$$\cos \theta = \frac{\text{length of side adjacent to } \theta}{\text{length of hypotenuse}}.$$

the tangent of θ, abbreviated to tan θ, is defined as

$$\tan \theta = \frac{\text{length of side opposite to } \theta}{\text{length of side adjacent to } \theta}.$$

α is the greek letter alpha and β beta.

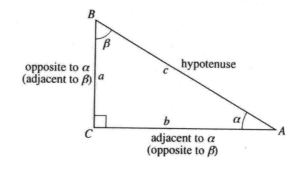

These definitions are exemplified below for the triangle ABC.

$$\sin \alpha = \frac{\text{opposite}}{\text{hypotenuse}} = \frac{a}{c}$$

$$\cos \alpha = \frac{\text{adjacent}}{\text{hypotenuse}} = \frac{b}{c}$$

Remember angles are sometimes in degrees and sometimes in radians and it is important to check which mode is being used when using a calculator.

$$\tan \alpha = \frac{\text{opposite}}{\text{adjacent}} = \frac{a}{b}$$

The hypotenuse is always the longest side (opposite the right-angle). The opposite and adjacent sides depend on the angle chosen. For example

$$\sin \beta = \frac{\text{opposite}}{\text{hypotenuse}} = \frac{b}{c}$$

Since sines, cosines, tangents, etc. are ratios of sides of triangles, those ratios are independent of the particular scale, and so depend only on the size of the angle. This means that the ratios of sides of a triangle can be used as a measure of angle.

Investigating trig ratios	Task 47

Find out how to switch your calculator between **degrees** and **radians**.

(a) Make sure that your calculator is in degree mode. Use it to investigate the sines, cosines and tangents of angles such as

0°, 30°, 45°, 60°, 90°, 120°, 150°, 163°, 180°, 199°.

Draw up a table to display your results.

Then try the same angles, but with a negative sign in front. Again use a table to display your results.

(b) Now switch your calculator to radian mode. Also find the key which is used to input π. Investigate the lines, cosines and tangents of angles in radians, such as:

0, 0.25, $\frac{\pi}{6}$, $\frac{\pi}{4}$, $\frac{4\pi}{3}$, 1.5, $\frac{\pi}{2}$, 2, π, 2π, 3π

and put the results in a table.

Try some investigations with the negatives of the same angles, and display those results as well.

Comment

You should have found that your calculator gives an answer for any value you have input with [sin] or [cos]. Calculators respond to angles of any size, even those greater than a complete turn (i.e., angles greater than 360° or 2π radians) or those in a negative direction (i.e., angles less than 0°).

However, some values used with [tan], such as 90° or $\pi/2$ radians, will have caused your calculator to give an error message. This is because the tangents of these angles are undefined.

Angles are conventionally measured counter-clockwise, a negative angle is one measured clockwise.

You may have noticed that some trigonometric ratios are the same for different angles: for example, sin 30° = sin 150° = 0.5.

The graph overleaf shows the values of sin$x$, cos$x$ and tan$x$ where x is between ⁻90° (-$\frac{\pi}{2}$) and 360° (2π).

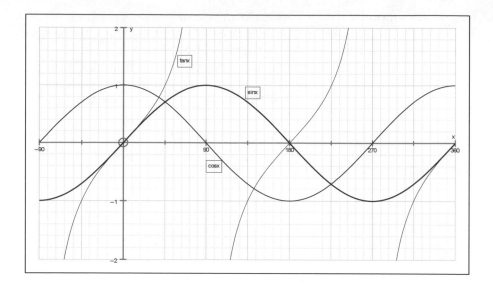

Task 48	Investigating in reverse

Set your calculator to degree mode and find the value of sin 30°. Now use the second function for this key $\boxed{\sin^{-1}}$ and see what happens. Can you describe the effect of using $\boxed{\sin^{-1}}$. Try some more values. Does the same thing happen? Try the other two trigonometric function keys $\boxed{\cos}$ and $\boxed{\tan}$ with $\boxed{\sin^{-1}}$ and $\boxed{\tan^{-1}}$. Does the same thing happen with them?

Now switch your calculator into radian mode and try the same thing again. Do you observe the same kind of effect?

Comment

The calculator gives sin 30° = 0.5 and using the second function returns $\sin^{-1}$ 0.5 = 30: $\sin^{-1}$ 'undoes' sin, and sin 'undoes' $\sin^{-1}$.

$\sin^{-1}$ 0.5 = 30 is interpreted as 'the angle whose sine is 0.5 is equal to 30°'.

You may have noticed that, for example, cos 300° = 0.5 but using the second function returns $\cos^{-1}$ 0.5 = 60. This is because the $\sin^{-1}$, $\cos^{-1}$ and $\tan^{-1}$ keys return angles in certain ranges.

The ranges are usually:

	From	To
$\sin^{-1}$	$^-90°\ (-\frac{\pi}{2})$	$90°\ (\frac{\pi}{2})$
$\cos^{-1}$	$0°(0)$	$180°(\pi)$
$\tan^{-1}$	$^-90°\ (-\frac{\pi}{2})$	$90°\ (-\frac{\pi}{2})$

So if you use $\boxed{\sin^{-1}}$ $\boxed{\cos^{-1}}$ or $\boxed{\tan^{-1}}$ in the middle of solving a problem, you may have to refer back to the problem to decide whether or not the answer given by the calculator is sensible, and adjust it, if necessary.

When using radian mode, the main difference that you are likely to notice is that, although you may have entered an angle as an expression involving π, the answer will always be returned as a decimal number. (You can check if a decimal number is a multiple of π by dividing by π.)

Knowledge of the trigonometric functions enables triangles to be 'solved'; that is, given some of the dimensions the others can usually be calculated. Although the ratios only apply to right-angled triangles, other triangles and figures can often be solved by constructing a perpendicular line.

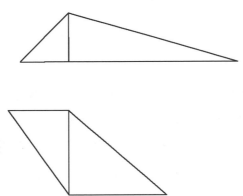

The trigonometrical ratios have practical applications, for example in finding heights (elevations).

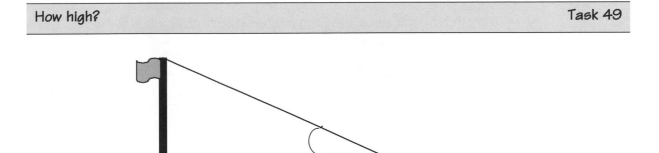

| How high? | Task 49 |

How could you work out the height of the flagpole in the diagram above if you knew the angle of elevation and the distance from the pole?

Comment

You know an angle and the adjacent length, so

$$\text{tan of the angle} \quad \frac{\text{height of pole}}{\text{distance from pole}}$$

(with both measurements being in the same units).

So height of the pole = distance from pole × tan of the angle.

Gradients

A similar problem to the pole height task is encountered when calculating the gradient of a stretch of road.

The ratios used in measuring the steepness of the slope of a road going up a hill are the same as two of the trigonometric ratios.

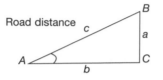

a = vertical height b = horizontal distance c = distance along road surface

A = angle of elevation

One measure of the steepness of a hill could be the angle of elevation; the larger the angle A the steeper the hill. But this angle cannot be measured on a map, and would need special equipment to measure on an actual road.

But the steepness, gradient, can be expressed in terms of the ratio of a pair of sides in the triangle representing the hill. The map method uses the ratio of the vertical distance to the horizontal distance, this gives:

$$\text{map gradient} = \frac{a}{b} = \frac{opposite}{adjacent} = \tan A$$

The method of calculating the map gradient corresponds to the mathematical definition of gradient:

$$\frac{\text{change in vertical height}}{\text{change in horizontal distance}}$$

The road method is the ratio of the vertical distance to the distance along the road surface (because that is easy to measure):

$$\text{road gradient} = \frac{a}{c} = \frac{opposite}{hypoteuse} = \sin A$$

The road gradient may be given as a fraction or a percentage: for example, a steep road gradient of 1/4 (1 in 4) is 25%, equivalent to an angle of elevation of approximately 15°.

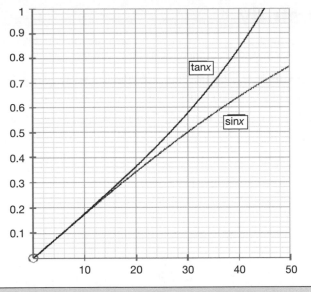

Roads for normal traffic range in steepness from flat to a maximum of 1:3.

What range of angles of elevation would this be?

Comment

Enlarging the graphs of sine and tangent, there is little difference in the values between 0° and 25°, so for car drivers the map gradient and the road gradient are, in effect, indistinguishable.

Mountain bikers prefer to use map gradients because the tangent of the angle of elevation is directly proportional to exertion required over the full range of hill slopes they can experience.

In mathematics gradients (tangents) are used as a measure of the steepness of straight line graphs and curves. For example the general equation of a straight line is $y = mx + c$ where m is the gradient of the line.

See Chapter 5.

Summary

Measures are used in order to make comparisons that may be either absolute or relative. One way of making comparisons 'fair' is to use ratios.

When making actual measurements consideration needs to be paid to:

- purpose;
- boundaries;
- accuracy and precision;
- units;
- appropriate tools.

Ratio is a fundamental mathematical concept which has a variety of applications within arithmetic, geometry, algebra and trigonometry.

Further study

Further details about units and measures are on the web site 'Dictionary of units and measurement' at: www.ex.ac.uk/cimt/dictunit/dictunit.htm (accessed 20 September 2006).

Graham, L. and Sargent, D. (1981) *Countdown to Mathematics*, volume 1, Prentice Hall.

Graham, L. and Sargent, D. (1981) *Countdown to Mathematics*, volume 2, Prentice Hall.

Countdown to Mathematics, volume 1 includes ratio and volume 2 trigonometry.

Stevens, S. (1946) 'On the theory of scales of measurement', *Science*, vol. 161, pp. 677–80.

4 Statistics

Introduction

This chapter is about handling quantitative information (otherwise known as data). It considers different types of data, explores ways that data can be processed, analysed and communicated and provides an introduction to some of the big ideas of statistics.

What is statistics?

The word 'statistics' is used to mean both numerical data (such as football results, so-called vital statistics of personal body measurements and so on) and the mathematically based discipline which is concerned with methods of collection, analysis and interpretation of data. In this latter sense, statistics provides an increasingly important way of describing and making sense of many aspects of the world.

Historically, the term 'statistics' derives from the collection of population data through censuses to be used by states for taxation purposes (literally, *state*-istics). Today, the use of statistics has broadened to include all areas of human activity. Data are collected on a vast scale, from individual shop purchases via till receipts and credit cards to world populations and many forms of scientific and social enquiry. However, as the following task shows, an isolated number fact on its own may not provide very helpful information.

Gee whiz, so what!   Task 51

Consider the following three statements and, for each one, list one or two additional 'background facts' you would like to know in order to make sense of them.

> The baby weighed 4.5 kg.

> The 8th runner finished in just under 7 hours.

> The average daily temperature was 35°C.

Comment

Your initial reaction might have been, 'Is that a lot or a little?' or perhaps, 'Is that good or bad?' Other information you might want could include, for example:

> How old was the baby?

How long was the race?

Where was it, and at what time of year?

To make any sense, these sorts of statements need to be placed in the context of similar data; for example, the usual range of weight for babies of that age, results of similar races and so on.

You might also have had questions about the source and accuracy of the facts.

To be fully informative, data need to be processed, analysed and interpreted; this is the role of statistics. There are usually considered to be four main phases in any statistical investigation or inquiry.

▶ Posing a question – specifying or identifying the purpose with a clearly stated question and working out ways of finding an answer.

▶ Collecting the data – implementing an experimental design for collecting new (primary) data or selecting existing (secondary) data from a suitable source.

▶ Analysing data (processing, summarising and representing) – typically this involves depicting the information graphically and using calculations to condense a lot of numbers into just one or two representative values.

▶ Interpreting results – using the information summaries to try to answer the original question.

These stages (PCAI) can be considered to be cyclic rather than linear in nature since any inquiry can result in raising further questions or modifying the original question which might require finding more data or re-processing existing data.

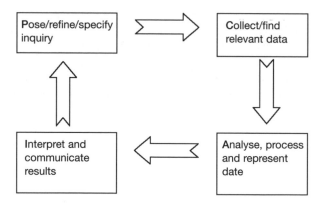

The rest of this chapter looks at some of the issues and techniques that tend to crop up in each of these stages.

Posing the question

The question posed in any inquiry determines everything that follows – for example, what are deemed to be relevant data, how this information can be collected and processed, and the way the results are interpreted and communicated. Learning statistical skills in isolation denies learners the opportunity of seeing and experiencing their purpose. It is a bit like spending hours on the piano practising scales but never getting to play a tune, or learning how to head, trap and pass a football but never playing a game.

Having said that, in order to save time and space, you will not be asked to pose questions for investigation yourself in this chapter. Because stage 'P' has not been included, some of the data you will need in this chapter will be supplied for you. Clearly, to some extent this contradicts the spirit of engaging in a purposeful statistical investigation as described above. However, the main job here is to set out the principles and techniques involved in the 'C', 'A' and 'I' stages of an investigation.

Collecting the data

Designing the questionnaire

Data can derive from various sources – for example, direct measurement (perhaps from an experiment), responses from a survey or data gleaned from other sources like books and newspapers. Where data are gathered from a survey, this may involve designing and administering a questionnaire. Questionnaire design is a large topic in its own right and cannot be explored at length here. However, here are a few simple guidelines for good questionnaire design.

Avoid asking questions that:

▶ you do not really need to know the answer to (this uses up valuable goodwill);

▶ cannot be answered (for example, 'How healthy are you?');

▶ may provide you with ambiguous responses that cannot easily be processed (for example, 'What are your views on education?');

▶ are likely to cause offence (for example, questions that are an unnecessary invasion of privacy);

▶ are biased (for example, 'Do you agree that murderous thugs should receive stiffer prison sentences?');

▶ include overlapping or missing categories in the options provided (for example, 'age categories: 0–20, 20–40, 40–60, etc.').

Choosing the sample

Like questionnaire design, sampling comprises many more issues than there is space to explore here. The need for sampling arises because

You will commonly see the word 'data' used either as a plural noun ('The data are gathered by questionnaire') or as a singular noun ('My data is stored on the computer'). In statistics 'data' is often used as a plural.

information may be wanted about a large number of people (or things) but it is not possible to contact them all. Many decisions in life are made on the basis of sampling. For example, you may want to check that your soup is exactly to your liking. Rather than drink it all, you taste a spoonful – a sample. To ensure that it is representative of the whole pot, you may give the soup a vigorous stir beforehand. Sampling in statistics is guided by two important principles. The sample should be:

- **representative** of the population from which it is taken. For example, sampling daytime shoppers may under-represent office workers, sampling just the people in a bus queue may under-represent car drivers, and so on;

- **sufficiently large** so as to provide meaningful results. For example, the newspaper journalist who based his headline on the voting intentions of five people he happened to ask in a pub has clearly failed on the 'sufficiently large sample size' principle.

Categories and measures

Data collection usually involves either putting the information into categories (names) or measuring on a scale. Think of the data taken by the police from a suspect. Some of the information they might wish to record is:

Name, Address, Sex, Age, Height, Hair colour, Eye colour, Shoe size.

Collecting these items of data sometimes involves putting in a category, and sometimes requires measuring. The next task will get you thinking about the difference between these two ways of recording information.

Task 52	Categories or measures?

Consider the following three out of the eight variables listed above:

Eye colour, Height, Shoe size.

Try to decide whether collecting these data involves using categories or measuring on a scale of measure.

Comment

A variable is an unknown quantity, or one that has a range of values.

Eye colour – and Name, Address, Sex and Hair colour – are categories. On the other hand, Height and Age are variables that you would measure on a scale.

Shoe size seems to fall between the two approaches. On the one hand it involves numbers, so might be listed under measuring. On the other hand, there is only a restricted number of shoe sizes available (you can only have whole and half sizes – you cannot have shoe size 7.1927, for example). So, in a sense, shoe sizes can be thought of as categories.

The most useful way of thinking about the various types of variables is to distinguish them as follows:

▶ where measurement is carried out on a continuous scale of measure the variable is called *continuous*;

▶ where categories are used (even where these are numbers, as with shoe size) the variable is called *discrete*.

These ways of classifying data are summarised below.

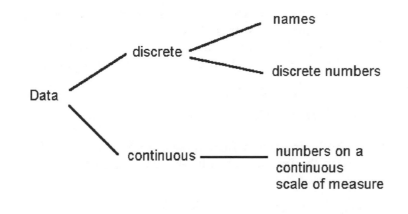

Look once more at the eight variables:

Name, Address, Sex, Age, Height, Hair colour, Eye colour, Shoe size.

(a) Which are numerical and which are names?

(b) Of the variables that are numbers, which are discrete and which continuous?

Comment

Age, Height and Shoe size are numerical, while the rest are names.

Shoe size is a discrete number variable, and Age and Height are continuous.

Note that although Age, like most measures of time, is a continuous variable, on a questionnaire most people will state their age rounded down to the full year below (someone who is 30 years and 7 months will say that they are 30 years old), so age data may actually be recorded as discrete numbers.

Analysing the data

In this section you will be shown some statistical graphs and calculations, based on the following two sets of mobile phone data.

Young children sometimes describe themselves as, say, 'aged $7\frac{3}{4}$'.

Data set 1: A group of students challenged their teachers to a speed-texting competition, using mobile phones. Each participant was timed as they keyed in and sent a standard message. The following data were generated.

Student times (secs): 33, 25, 19, 24, 41, 30, 21, 24, 29, 27, 19, 30.

Teacher times (secs): 31, 18, 51, 27, 33, 36, 47, 28, 33.

(*Source*: Graham 2006, p. 82)

Looking at the raw data alone, you cannot easily get a clear sense of overall patterns and differences. It is difficult even to see how many people there are in each category. As a first step to making the data easier to handle, it is often a good idea to the sort the data into order, thus:

Student times (secs): 19, 19, 21, 24, 24, 25, 27, 29, 30, 30, 33, 41.

Teacher times (secs): 18, 27, 28, 31, 33, 33, 36, 47, 51.

Data set 2: The students and teachers made a note of their phone manufacturer, with the following results (Nokia = N, Motorola = M, Sony = S, O_2 = O).

Student phones: N, N, M, O, O, O, N, S, S, N, N, N.

Teacher phones: M, S, S, S, O, N, S, M, S.

To get a clearer sense of the data it is often useful to use the strategy of *visualising*. With statistics this usually involves drawing graphs and diagrams.

Graphing the data

Knowing which graph or diagram to draw is not always obvious – the choice depends partly on the nature of the data and also on the sort of analysis you want to make.

Here are the more common graphs in use:

pie chart, bar chart, histogram, boxplot, line graph, scatterplot.

These days, graphs can be drawn easily, using a machine – a computer spreadsheet or graphics calculator, for example. Letting the machine do the mechanical part enables you to put your energies where they are most usefully directed: in thinking about which type of graph would be most helpful in meeting your needs, and in interpreting the graph once it has been drawn.

Not all of the graph types given above can be used to represent either of these two data sets (for example, the last two, line graph and scatterplot, would be inappropriate). You will find out later why this is the case. Based on what you may already know about these graphs, Task 54 asks you to match the first three types of graphs to the two data sets above.

Look in turn at the four types of graph listed below and, for each one, try to imagine how you could use it to depict data set 1 and data set 2.

   Pie chart, bar chart, histogram.

Where you hit a problem, try to think through what the problem is.

Comment

More details are provided later in this chapter, when you have had a chance to think more carefully about the nature of these graphs and how and when they are drawn.

For now, look at the three sets of graphs on page 80, the pie chart, bar chart and histogram. Although it is technically possible to use all of these to depict both data sets, some are more appropriate than others. The choices made below represent sensible choices in matching graph to data type. Try to decide how helpful they are in the context of possible questions you might want to ask of the data and what sort of conclusions can be drawn from them. These issues will be taken up again in the next section, 'Interpreting the results'.

Pie charts

In order to represent data set 2 as two pie charts, it is helpful to summarise the information in a table, as follows:

	Students	Teachers
Nokia	6	1
O_2	3	1
Sony	2	5
Motorola	1	2

Based on this summary, pie charts of the mobile phone type data are shown overleaf.

With a pie chart, the size of each sector is a measure of its frequency. In the student pie chart above, the sector marked Nokia is the largest, reflecting the fact that Nokia is the most common manufacturer for these students. For the pie chart of teacher phone types, the Sony sector is largest. Note a useful convention used when drawing pie charts, which has been adopted in the student pie chart – the sectors are placed in decreasing order of size, working clockwise from the 12 o'clock position. This makes it easier to spot the largest and the smallest categories at a glance. For reasons of consistency, the same ordering of categories has been used for the teacher chart.

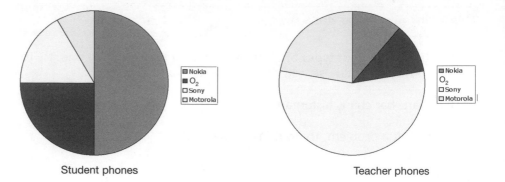

Student phones   Teacher phones

One issue that is masked by these depictions is that the two pies are shown to be the same size when in fact there were more students than teachers (12 compared with 9). This could be taken account of by scaling down the teacher pie chart so that its *area* is three-quarters that of the students chart. However, scaling would make no difference to the appearance of the subdivisions of this pie chart – it is just a matter of adjusting its size.

Bar charts

Below are bar charts based on the data set 2.

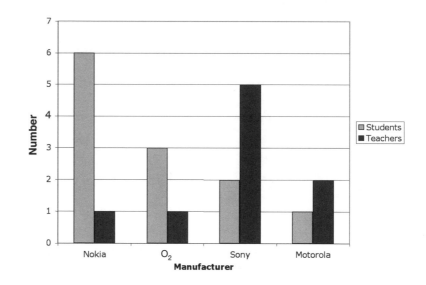

A problem with this particular graph is that, because you started with 12 students and only 9 teachers, it is inevitable that the student bars will tend to be taller than those of the teachers, which can give a misleading impression. A way of dealing with this problem is to recalculate the data based on the *proportions* in each category. This information is summarised in the table overleaf.

	Students (%)	Teachers (%)
Nokia	50	11
O_2	25	11
Sony	17	56
Motorola	8	22

The corresponding percentage bar chart is shown below. Note that the vertical axis has now been re-labelled to indicate this adjustment.

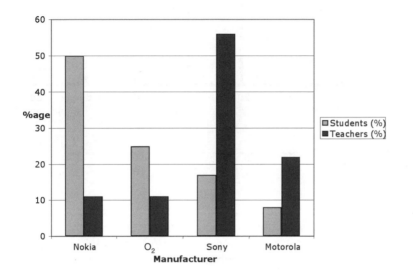

With bar charts (sometimes known as column graphs), the tallest bar corresponds to the category that occurred most frequently. The bars on a bar chart can be drawn either vertically (as is the case above) or horizontally.

Histograms

Like a bar chart, a histogram is a form of block graph. The distinction between a histogram and a bar chart is to do with the sort of data they represent. Whereas a bar chart is used to represent discrete data (i.e., categories or discrete numbers), a histogram represents continuous data (for example, people's heights, weights, ages, texting times and so on). This distinction shows up visually according to whether or not there are gaps between adjacent bars: a bar chart should have these gaps (to emphasise the discrete nature of the data) whereas a histogram should be drawn so that adjacent bars touch (to emphasise the continuous nature of the data).

As data set 1 consists of times, which are a continuous measure, a histogram is an appropriate form of representation, and this is shown below for the student and teacher data combined (21 people in all).

Note: the two data sets were combined here simply to create a sufficiently large data set to give the resulting histogram an interesting overall shape. Drawing histograms based on very small data sets tends to produce rather flat, uninteresting representations which yield few interesting patterns.

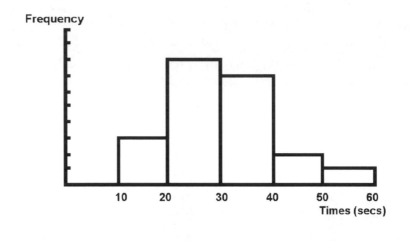

Task 55	Observing data

Examine the different graphs above and make a note of some conclusions that you could draw from them. These might include such remarks as: the most/least common mobile phone manufacturers, how widely spread out the texting times are, the general distribution of texting times and so on.

Comment

Here are some of the observations you might have made:

From the pie charts it is fairly easy to see that the students favoured Nokia phones whereas the teachers preferred Sony models. The bar chart displayed the same information but it also made it easy for your eye to make direct comparisons between the types of phones used by the two groups. The histogram shows how the majority of times are concentrated in the 20–40-second range and a lower density at the two extremes.

There is another type of graph, a boxplot, which is particularly useful for giving an indication of how widely spread the data are. It is included in the later section, 'Calculating the spread' p. 85.

Graphs give a good visual impression of the data, but often more detailed or precise summaries are needed. These are found from the data by calculation. The most common sorts of calculation are finding an average (as a measure of a typical value) and finding a measure of how spread out the data are.

Calculating averages

There are three common averages: the mean, mode and median.

The mean

The arithmetic mean is the most commonly used average and is the one most people are probably referring to when they talk about 'the average'. The mean is the sum of all the observations divided by the number of observations. So, to calculate the mean of, the nine teachers' texting times and the 12 student times:

> Teacher mean = (18 + 27 + 28 + 31 + 33 + 33 + 36 + 47 + 51)/9 = 271/9 = 33.9 secs
> Student mean = (19 + 19 + 21 + 24 + 24 + 25 + 27 + 29 + 30 + 30 + 33 + 41)/12 = 322/12 = 26.8 secs

Both of these mean values have been rounded to 1 decimal place.

Note that, using a spreadsheet, the function '=AVERAGE' can be used to calculate the mean of a list of numbers.

Thinking around the mean	Task 56

Suppose that someone calculates the mean texting times of 14 students and you are told that the answer comes to 26.8 seconds (rounded to one decimal place). You then discover that they missed out one student and this 15th time was 41 seconds. How can you use this information to make a good estimate of the mean time for all 15 students?

Comment

In order to find the mean time for all 15 students, you need the total and then divide by 15. This is done as follows.

> The total for the original 14 students = 14 × 26.8 = 375 secs (approximately).

> The total for all 15 students = 375 + 41 = 416 secs.

> The mean for all 15 students = 416/15 = 27.7 secs (to 1 decimal place).

A useful rough check on whether you calculated the mean correctly is that your answer should lie somewhere between the smallest (minimum) value and the largest (maximum) value of the data. If the calculated mean lies outside this range, it is clearly wrong. Because the mean is found as a result of performing a division calculation, its value will almost always be a decimal number and you must decide to what degree of accuracy to round the answer. The usual convention is to round to one decimal place of accuracy greater than the accuracy of the raw data.

In the example given here, the raw data were collected as whole numbers (i.e., zero decimal places) and so the mean was given to one decimal place.

The mode

The mode applies to data where certain values or categories recur. The mode is the value or category that occurs most frequently. If, say, the heights of 20 people were measured to the nearest millimetre, it is quite possible that everyone would have a different height, in which case the mode could not be used. A way around this problem could be to group the heights into broader bands (perhaps into 2 cm intervals). The mode would then apply to the interval that contained the greatest number of people, in which case it would be termed the *modal interval*.

Unlike the mean, the mode need not be restricted to numbers. For example, a company might carry out a survey on how staff travel to work and come up with results like these.

How staff usually travel to work

Car	28
Bus	9
Train	14
Bicycle	19
Walk	16

From these sorts of data, only the mode will produce a useful summary – the modal form of transport is the car. For the student phone data, the Nokia is the modal category for the students and the Sony is the modal category for the teachers.

As was the case with the mean, the mode should lie within the range of data values. But, unlike the mean, the mode must be one of the members of the data set. So, if the data consist only of whole numbers, the mode must also be a whole number.

The median

The median of a set of values is found by sorting the data into order and selecting the middle value.

In data set 1, there are nine numbers in the teacher times, so here the median is the fifth value when sorted into order. A small complication arises when finding the median of the student times. Because there is an even number of values here, there would be no single middle one. In such cases, the remedy is to choose the **two** middle values, i.e., the sixth and seventh, when sorted in order, and the median is the number midway between these numbers (i.e., the mean of these two numbers).

Calculate the median of the two sets of times listed in data set 1.

Comment

There are 9 teachers' times recorded in data set 1, so the median is the value of the fifth time, when sorted in order, which is 33 seconds.

There are 12 student times, so the median is calculated as halfway between the sixth and the seventh time, when sorted in order. This equals (25 + 27)/2 = 26 seconds.

Calculating the spread

Just as there are several ways of measuring averages (the mean, mode and median), there are different measures which show how widely spread the values are. The most common are the range, the interquartile range, and the standard deviation. In this section only the first two of these will be covered.

The range is the difference between the largest and the smallest value in the data set. For example, in data set 1:

the range of student times = 41 seconds – 19 seconds = 22 seconds.

One problem with the range is that it can easily be affected by an untypical value. For example, suppose one of the students was timed at, say 150 seconds. Because of this one highly unrepresentative value, the range would increase from 22 seconds to 131 seconds (i.e., 150 seconds – 19 seconds), which would give a misleading impression.

One way around this is to create a new measure of spread which uses the range between two values that are not quite at the extremes. The interquartile range measures the range of the middle half of the values. It is the difference between the values of the upper quartile and the lower quartile. These two quartiles are the values of the numbers that are one-quarter of the way in from either end of the data set, once the data set has been sorted in order of size. If there are 12 values, the lower quartile is, roughly speaking, the value of the third number, while the upper quartile is, approximately, the value of the tenth number.

It is possible to be more precise than this in defining a quartile but textbooks vary slightly as to how it is defined. It is enough here to know that, in order to find the quartiles, you must first sort the data and then find the two values that are approximately one-quarter of the way in from each end.

For the 12 student times in data set 1, the third and tenth values are approximately in the correct position. For the 9 teacher times in data set 1 the quartiles are trickier to find. A reasonable approximation is to place the lower quartile at a position halfway between the second and third values and the upper quartile halfway between the seventh and eighth values.

Thus, for the 12 student times:

lower quartile, Q1 = 21 seconds and upper quartile, Q3 = 30 seconds;

student interquartile range = Q3 – Q1 = 30 seconds – 21 seconds = 9 seconds.

Task 58	Calculating the spread

Calculate the range and the interquartile ranges of the nine teacher times in data set 1.

Comment

Range of teacher times = 51 seconds – 18 seconds = 33 seconds.

The lower quartile for teachers is roughly halfway between the second and third value when sorted in order. So, Q1 = (27 + 28)/2 = 27.5 seconds.

The upper quartile for teachers is roughly halfway between the seventh and eighth value when sorted in order. So, Q3 = (36 + 47)/2 = 41.5 seconds.

So, the interquartile range = Q3 – Q1 = 41.5 seconds – 27.5 seconds = 14 seconds.

Boxplots (box and whiskers diagrams)

As was explained earlier, a set of raw data is difficult to interpret and the summary calculations given above provide a useful overview of the sort of values it contains. Working from smallest to biggest, five of the most useful of these summary values are:

minimum value, lower quartile, median, upper quartile, maximum value.

Boxplots and other novel representations like 'stem and leaf' diagrams were first popularised by John Tukey in America in the 1970s.

These five summary values can be represented in a type of graph called a boxplot (sometimes referred to as a 'box and whiskers' diagram). The boxplots below depict the text times from data set 1. This is a screen picture created on a TI-84 Plus graphics calculator.

The upper boxplot in the figure shows the five-figure summary of the 12 student times; the lower boxplot corresponds to the 9 teacher times. The diagram below spells out the positions of each value of a general boxplot.

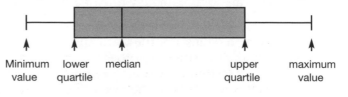

| Minimum value | lower quartile | median | upper quartile | maximum value |

The strength of the boxplot is that it reveals, at a glance, the key features of a set of data. For example, the central box marks out the interquartile range.

The lengths of the left and right whiskers indicate how widely spread the lower and upper quarters of the data are. The width of the central box indicates the spread of the middle 50% of the values. When two or more boxplots are drawn one below the other on the same scale, direct comparisons can be made between the data batches. For example, from the boxplots of the student and teacher texting times you can see that, in general, student times are lower than those of the teachers but that the spread of teacher times is greater. You can also see that, although one teacher was faster than all the students, half the students were faster than the lower quartile time of the teachers.

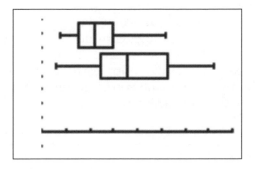

Interpreting the results

Typically at stage **A** of a statistical investigation (analysing the data) you draw various graphs and perform a variety of summary calculations (for example, finding the mean, median or interquartile range). Not all of these would necessarily be particularly helpful and so in a 'real' investigation you would focus just on those calculations and graphs which might reveal insights into the data. The **I** stage is where these graphs and summaries are interpreted in the light of the question posed in the original problem.

Drawing conclusions	Task 59

On the basis of the calculations and graphs used with data set 1, what conclusions are you able to draw about student and teacher texting times?

Comment

It should be stressed that it would be dangerous to attempt to use these results as a basis for drawing general conclusions about all teachers and all students – the sample sizes (9 and 12, respectively) are too small for such an inference to be made and there has been no attempt to check how representative these two groups of people are of the wider category of 'all students' and 'all teachers'. However, for these two sets of people, there are some fairly clear differences. The mean and median student times are considerably lower than for the teachers but the student spreads are narrower. The two boxplots confirm this impression.

Knowing which average and graph to use

It is one thing to know how to calculate the various averages and draw a variety of graphs, but it is quite another to know when their use is most appropriate. A major problem with learning statistical techniques merely as a set of skills to no real purpose is that, out of context, appropriateness of use simply does not arise. As has already been mentioned earlier in the chapter, making an intelligent choice about which to use is most likely to happen in the context of a real (or plausible) statistical investigation. This section looks at the pros and cons of the different averages and graphs.

Knowing which average to use

A way of deciding which average to use is to ask: 'Does this average help me to answer my question?' The choice of average will be affected by the precise wording of the question under consideration. For example, if you wished to know what a typical teacher earns, then you might choose the median salary, whereas the most common earnings would require the mode. The next activity will provide you with some contexts in which to practise your skills in choosing a suitable average.

Task 60	Which average?

In a survey, each respondent was asked to record information on a variety of factors. Which average would you choose to summarise the following?

(a) Country of origin

(b) Lucky number

(c) Date of birth

(d) Weight

(e) Household size

Comment

The preferred choice of average and brief explanations are given in the table below.

Example	Preferred average	Comment
(a) Country of origin	Mode	As the data are non-numerical, only the mode will do.
(b) Lucky number	Mode	Although these data are numerical, it makes no sense to find the mean or median.

Example	Preferred average	Comment
(c) Date of birth	Possibly mode	Again, it makes no sense to find the mean or median here. The mode might be useful but only if the data were grouped into months or by star sign – it depends on what you want to investigate.
(d) Weight	Mean or median	Which of these you choose will depend on whether you want to know the 'average' weight (the mean) or what a typical person weighs (the median).
(e) Household size	Mean, median, mode	All three are possible, and which you choose will depend on context. Note that calculating the mean may produce a value such as 4.7. Although such a value is impossible to get for a given household, it is meaningful to refer to the average in terms of a non-integer value. Choose the median if you want the household size for the average person. Choose the mode if you want the most common household size.

Knowing which graph to use

Like the averages, the graphs are suitable for different purposes and each illustrates some features of the data and ignores others. Before you read on, you may like to look over the graphs you have met so far and make notes on their strengths and weaknesses.

Pie charts

In general, a pie chart is drawn so that the size of each slice matches the number of occurrences of that category. In the pie charts on page 80, the size of each slice of the pie corresponds to the number of people who own that particular make of mobile phone.

A pie chart is suitable only for representing a single batch of discrete, categorical data. It is also not recommended for numerical data. One reason for this is that having the number categories arranged in a circle is less helpful than if they are arranged on a straight line (you end up with a large number placed alongside a smaller number, which is a bit silly!). Also it can be confusing when trying to represent empty categories as these simply disappear.

A very important feature of a pie chart is that the complete pie should represent something meaningful (the left-hand pie on page 80 represents the phone models of all 12 students in the survey). Also, be careful if you are using two pies to represent data from two different-sized data sets. Ideally, the pies should be drawn so that the area of each pie matches its size – something that is very difficult to do using a computer. However, in general, pie charts are not very helpful for comparing two sets of data.

Bar charts
Like the pie chart, a bar chart is suitable only for representing discrete data. The bar chart on page 80 shows clearly the pattern of phone ownership for the students and teachers and is a good choice here. For example, the tallest bar shows the mode, while the heights of the bars show how frequently the phone models occurred.

Histograms
As was mentioned earlier, histograms are suitable only for depicting continuous data, whereas bar charts should be reserved for discrete data. Technically, it is the area (rather than the height) of each bar that indicates its frequency. In practice, this is not a problem when the intervals of the bars are equal but if you should wish to introduce the complication of unequal bar widths, then the height of each bar will need to be adjusted to take account of its width.

For a more detailed explanation of how to do this, see Graham (2003, Ch. 3).

Investigations using paired data

The investigation of texting times and phone ownership provided suitable contexts for introducing a range of different calculations and graphs, but two types of graph – the line graph and the scatterplot – were not covered. The reason is that the use of these graphs is not appropriate for the sort of data that were provided in data sets 1 and 2. The line graph and scatterplot are used to represent paired data and are useful in investigating relationships between two things.

Line graph
The table below gives the heights of a child taken every year between the ages of 6 and 16 years.

Heights of a child between the ages of 6 and 16 years

Age (years)	6	7	8	9	10	11
Height (cm)	109	111	118	121	125	130
Age (years)	12	13	14	15	16	
Height (cm)	133	148	159	161	161	

Below is a line graph depicting these data:

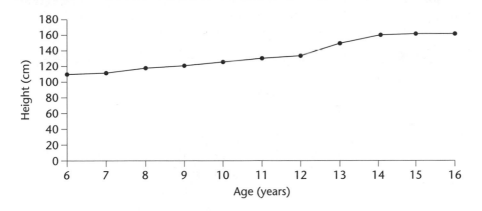

The steeper parts of the graph indicate this child's growth spurts. The graph levels out at around the age of 14 or 15 years when the child stopped growing.

Drawing the line graph differently

In drawing line graphs you (or the computer) choose the scales. You may have wondered how much it matters what scales you use in terms of how it affects the appearance of the graph. The next task explores this question by looking at some ways of redrawing the line graph above.

Redrawing the line graph	Task 61

Consider the following three features of the line graph.

▶ There is a lot space below a height of 1 metre. Version A below has been redrawn so that the vertical axis begins at 100 cm.

▶ You may have wondered whether the graph could be drawn with the two axes interchanged. This is version B.

▶ The horizontal scale has been squashed up. This is version C.

Do the three versions overleaf seem valid ways of representing the data? If not, then why not?

Comment

Version A: there is no problem with chopping the vertical or horizontal axes but, if possible, it is a good idea to indicate that you have done so by drawing a little break in the axis as shown opposite.

However, this is difficult to achieve when the graph is created on computer, so the reader needs to check carefully the scales on both axes.

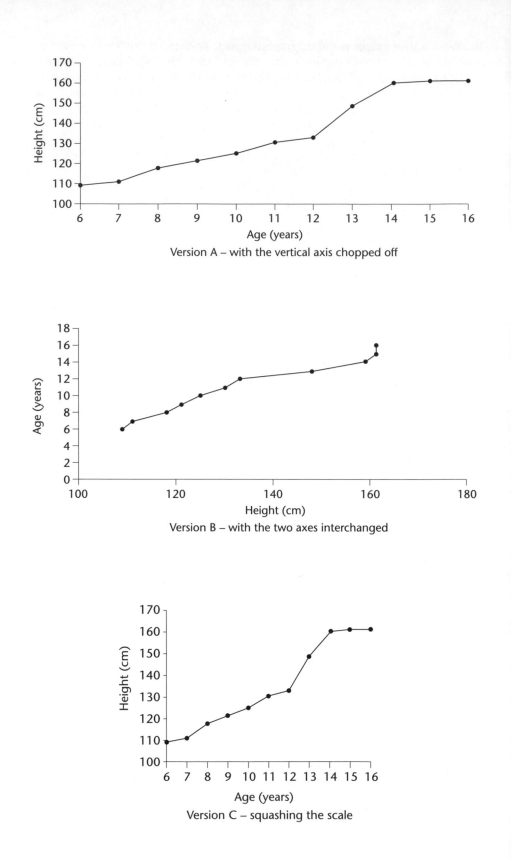

Version A – with the vertical axis chopped off

Version B – with the two axes interchanged

Version C – squashing the scale

Version B: unfortunately, this is simply wrong. An agreed convention when drawing graphs of paired data is that the 'independent' variable is placed on the horizontal axis and 'dependent' variable on the vertical axis. A way of deciding which is which is to say to yourself: 'Does a child's height depend on her age, or does her age depend on her height?' Clearly the answer is the former, and so height is the dependent variable, Height, should therefore be placed on the vertical axis. If Time is one of the variables being depicted, it is usually placed on the horizontal axis for the obvious reason that the passing of time is independent of anything else.

There may be situations where it is not clear which variable is dependent on which; in such cases the choice of axes probably does not matter too much!

Version C: This graph is actually correct, but notice how this squashing changes the slope of the line.

Overall, beware of jumping to conclusions if a graph appears to rise or fall very steeply. This effect can be created artificially by chopping the vertical axis or altering the scales.

Bar chart or line graph?

If the data being displayed are discrete (i.e., are either discrete numbers or categories), drawing a chart where the values are joined up as a line graph is inappropriate. In general, line graphs are used to represent continuous data. Only join up the values on a graph if the lines between the points make sense. The two graphs below, showing a survey of pet ownership taken from a class of students, illustrate this.

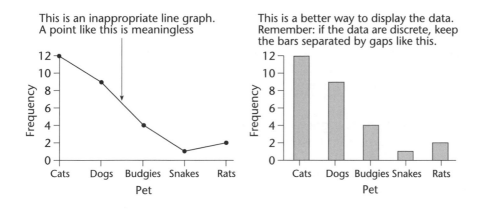

Scatterplot

In a psychological experiment, a volunteer, Irene, was shown photographs of 25 people of widely varying ages and asked to guess the age of each person. The researcher then used a scatterplot, plotting Irene's guesses on the vertical axis and the actual ages on the horizontal axis. This is shown overleaf.

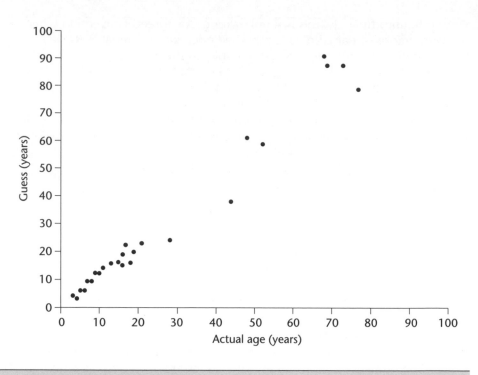

Task 62	Ages and ages

(a) Describe the main features of this scatterplot.

(b) What does it tell you about the relationship between the two variables in question?

Comment

The points lie in roughly a straight line, running from bottom left to top right of the graph. In other words, the higher the actual age, the higher was Irene's guess. There is therefore a positive relationship between the two variables.

The pattern of points suggests that her guesses were quite good. Imagine a straight line drawn from the origin (i.e., the point with Actual age = 0 and Guess = 0) to the point with Actual age = 80 and Guess = 80. Such a line goes through all points where the guess was the same as the actual age and therefore represents a set of perfect guesses. A measure of how good Irene's guesses were is to see how far the crosses on the scatterplot lie from this imaginary line. Also, you can see at a glance whether Irene has a tendency to overestimate (indicated by points above the line) or underestimate (points below the line). A third feature worth noting is that the majority of the points are concentrated in the lower left part of the graph, indicating that the majority of these 25 people were quite young. Bearing this in mind, was Irene better at estimating the ages of younger or older people?

Summary

This chapter looked at some important statistical ideas.

▶ Statistical information (data) needs to be seen in context in order for it to be understood and used sensibly.

▶ To aid the purposeful learning of statistics, it is useful to refer to the following four headings – posing questions (P), collecting data (C), analysing data (A) and interpreting the results (I). These four stages, which can be usefully thought of as a cycle, are referred to by the acronym PCAI.

▶ At the 'C' stage of the PCAI acronym, it is useful to learn about good questionnaire design and sampling.

▶ At the 'A' stage, it is useful to be able to summarise data (using averages and measures of spread) and to be able to represent the data graphically (using pie charts, bar charts, histograms, boxplots, scatterplots and line graphs).

▶ Still at the 'A' stage, thought needs to be given to matching the various statistical tools to purposes and to types of data.

At the 'I' stage is useful to be reminded what started the investigation off in the first place and to check that you have answered the initial question.

Further study

Graham, A. (2003) *Teach Yourself Statistics*, Hodder & Stoughton. *Teach Yourself Statistics* covers basic statistics including uses in everyday life.

Graham, A. (2006) *Developing Thinking in Statistics*, Paul Chapman Publishing. *Developing Thinking in Statistics* is a broader treatment of the 'big ideas' in statistics including using ICT for teaching and learning.

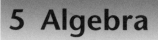

5 Algebra

Introduction

For many people, the word 'algebra' conjures up a forest of letters, numbers and symbols, and a memory of apparently pointless rules for doing things with expressions and solving equations. This is similar to having the impression that cooking is only about following complicated recipes using special techniques. It misses the point about algebra, its power and simplicity.

'Algebra is an attribute, a fundamental power of the mind. Not of mathematics only.' (Gattegno, 1977)

Algebra is about generalised mathematical thinking arising from seeing patterns and relationships. It is about expressing those patterns in words, symbols, diagrams and graphs, and interpreting what is observed. The important patterns are those that are not just particular to one situation, but are generalisations that apply to many different situations that have underlying similarities. Expressing these perceived generalities is the root of algebra, which is why algebra is also concerned with:

▶ expressing the same thing in different forms;

▶ doing and undoing.

This chapter is in five main sections, all of which are aspects of algebra:

▶ *finding and using pattern* — saying and recording what is seen in different ways;

▶ *generalised arithmetic* — becoming explicitly aware of the rules for manipulating numbers;

▶ *finding the unknown* — using a symbol to stand for an as-yet-unknown quantity, which can be used to form and solve equations;

▶ *using formulas* — formulas as shorthand, and using them to find values;

▶ *picturing functions* — representing functions as equations, tables and graphs.

Finding and using pattern

Generality is an important part of mathematics. The most basic and clear instance is in pattern spotting, in seeing links and connections between things. This section takes a simple situation and uses it to demonstrate several of the processes of algebraic thinking, including becoming aware of a pattern and expressing it in words, pictures and symbols.

Identifying and expressing generality

Although 'seeing' a pattern is often talked about, visualising a pattern in your head is not the only way of being aware of it. You may find a pattern more obvious when spoken; or you may prefer to draw diagrams or use words and symbols. These are all important ways of expressing patterns and you can improve your algebraic thinking by being able to move between them. The following tasks are designed to help you gain confidence in doing this.

| Shady circles | Task 63 |

In the first block below, shade in every third circle starting from the second counting left to right, row by row.

○ ○ ○ ○ ○ ○ ○ ○   ○ ○ ○ ○ ○ ○ ○ ○   ○ ○ ○ ○ ○ ○ ○ ○
○ ○ ○ ○ ○ ○ ○ ○   ○ ○ ○ ○ ○ ○ ○ ○   ○ ○ ○ ○ ○ ○ ○ ○
○ ○ ○ ○ ○ ○ ○ ○   ○ ○ ○ ○ ○ ○ ○ ○   ○ ○ ○ ○ ○ ○ ○ ○
○ ○ ○ ○ ○ ○ ○ ○   ○ ○ ○ ○ ○ ○ ○ ○   ○ ○ ○ ○ ○ ○ ○ ○
○ ○ ○ ○ ○ ○ ○ ○   ○ ○ ○ ○ ○ ○ ○ ○   ○ ○ ○ ○ ○ ○ ○ ○
○ ○ ○ ○ ○ ○ ○ ○   ○ ○ ○ ○ ○ ○ ○ ○   ○ ○ ○ ○ ○ ○ ○ ○
○ ○ ○ ○ ○ ○ ○ ○   ○ ○ ○ ○ ○ ○ ○ ○   ○ ○ ○ ○ ○ ○ ○ ○
○ ○ ○ ○ ○ ○ ○ ○   ○ ○ ○ ○ ○ ○ ○ ○   ○ ○ ○ ○ ○ ○ ○ ○
○ ○ ○ ○ ○ ○ ○ ○   ○ ○ ○ ○ ○ ○ ○ ○   ○ ○ ○ ○ ○ ○ ○ ○
○ ○ ○ ○ ○ ○ ○ ○   ○ ○ ○ ○ ○ ○ ○ ○   ○ ○ ○ ○ ○ ○ ○ ○
○ ○ ○ ○ ○ ○ ○ ○   ○ ○ ○ ○ ○ ○ ○ ○   ○ ○ ○ ○ ○ ○ ○ ○
○ ○ ○ ○ ○ ○ ○ ○   ○ ○ ○ ○ ○ ○ ○ ○   ○ ○ ○ ○ ○ ○ ○ ○
○ ○ ○ ○ ○ ○ ○ ○   ○ ○ ○ ○ ○ ○ ○ ○   ○ ○ ○ ○ ○ ○ ○ ○

Comment

Many people find that at some point they shift from counting to following pattern. At first, they are not confident of the pattern and so keep counting, but then the pattern takes over. If you did not notice this happening, try another version on the second block: shade in every fifth circle starting with the third.

| More shady circles | Task 64 |

On a fresh block, shade in every third circle starting from the second, but this time counting from left to right in the first row, then right to left in the second, and so on, weaving your way down the rows. Look out for where your brain moves from counting to having confidence in the pattern. Try to say what happened.

Comment

These tasks illustrate the power most people have for seeking out and employing patterns. The tasks started with a given counting rule, 'shade in every ...' but in doing the task the brain simplified it to something like 'lines are developing' and 'just continue the lines ...'.

Task 63 and Task 64 were concerned with *seeing* a pattern. To reach generality you need to be able to *express* a pattern in words and symbols. How you do this is closely connected with the particular way in which you see the pattern. The following tasks take you through the process of expressing generality arising from a sequence of diagrams.

Task 65	Brick wall

Imagine a brick wall being built. The sequence of pictures below show stages in building a two-layer wall.

Notice what you see, and say to yourself how the sequence is being built up – what stays the same and what changes.

Comment

As has been said, the particular way you noticed the pattern developing will have determined what you said. However, the pattern can be 'seen' in different ways. Here are three of the many different ways of 'seeing' and 'saying' the brick sequence.

Notice that these diagrams are in two-dimensions – the three-dimensions of actual bricks have been ignored. This is easier to draw, but also stresses the changes in the sequence.

'One brick, and then one brick with one pair of bricks added on, then one with two pairs added on, one with three pairs added on, ...'

'There are two rows, the top row having one brick less than the bottom row. The bottom row has one, two, three, ... bricks in it, ... The number on the bottom is the same as its position in the sequence.'

'One brick, three bricks, five bricks, seven bricks, ... This fits the odd numbers, and is going up in twos.'

That there are several different ways of expressing the same brick pattern suggests that there is an underlying generality.

Choose one of the ways of 'seeing and saying' the brick pattern, work out the 37th in the sequence. How many bricks would there be?

Comment

Taking the second way of seeing you might produce something like:

Picture number 37 in the sequence will have two rows of bricks. There will be 37 bricks in the bottom row, and one less (36) bricks in row two – so there are 73 altogether.

This could be shortened to:

Picture 37 needs 37 (bottom row) + 36 (top row) bricks, so 73 altogether.

Algebraic thinking has already begun.

Alternatively, if you had recalled the connection with the sequence of numbers worked on in Chapter 1, you might have remembered (or looked up) that to find a particular odd number 'double the position in the sequence and subtract one'. So the 37th is:

$(2 \times 37) - 1 = 74 - 1$, making 73 bricks.

I have a 'picture number' in my head.

Using the second way of seeing the brick sequence, say out loud how to calculate the number of bricks in the picture.

Now try to write down the instructions. How will you convince yourself that your solution works?

Comment

You might have said something like:

Whatever 'picture number' you are thinking of, add it to one less.

This question is the heart of the 'expressing generality' aspect of algebra.

You may have felt that producing a general statement was more challenging than producing the 37th number, because of the difficulty of finding a way of referring to an unknown number. You may even have felt that you could have used symbols.

Recording in different forms

When starting to record algebra symbolically some people like to refer to the unknown by drawing a little cloud ☁, or 'thinks bubble' for 'the number in your head', or □, to indicate a box into which the number can be put. Others do not find clouds or boxes helpful, and prefer words, such as 'picture number', or letters, such as p. Using letters is certainly neither obvious nor automatic; using clouds or empty boxes may provide a stronger image of an as-yet-unknown.

The following are some ways of recording the number of bricks in a general picture in the brick sequence.

▶ The number of bricks in any brick picture is the total of the picture number and one less than the picture number.

▶ Number of bricks = ☁ add ☁ take away 1.

▶ Number of bricks = □ plus □ less 1.

▶ Number of bricks = (picture number) plus (picture number –1).

▶ Number of bricks = $p + (p - 1)$ which is the same as 2p – 1.

Each of these statements says the same thing; and they each have strengths and weaknesses.

Task 68	Different forms of recording

Think about the advantages and disadvantages of each of the above methods of recording the number of bricks in a general picture.

Comment

The word statement retains the meaning but its wordiness may make it difficult to follow. The statements using symbols are shorter to write but drawing the pictures is a bit laborious. The expression using p is succinct and so easy to write, but because it is so concise it may need more interpreting. It does have one very important advantage: it is the easiest to simplify. The expression $p + (p - 1)$ is $p + p - 1$ which simplifies to $2p - 1$, which is an even more concise form.

The instructions for calculating the number of bricks could be written as a mathematical formula:

$$b = 2p - 1$$

where b is the number of bricks and p is the picture number in the sequence.

The steps in generating a rule for a sequence can be summarised as follows.

▸ Say how you see the pattern continuing, and try to identify other ways of seeing it.

▸ For each way of seeing, state a rule or method for generating the sequence.

▸ Decide how a general picture can be built, and use it to find a systematic way of counting.

▸ Express your way of counting, perhaps first in pictures or words, then in some shortened form, perhaps as a mathematical formula.

What is next? Task 69

Look at the following sequences of numbers. In each case predict the value of the next three terms (numbers).

(a) 3, 6, 9, 12, …

(b) 4, 7, 10, 13, …

Then try to work out the general rule for the value of the nth term.

Comment

(a) 15, 18, 21. You should have noticed that the numbers given are the start of the 3 times table. So the value of the nth term will be $3n$.

(b) 16, 19, 22. Each term is one more than those in the previous example, so the nth term would be $3n + 1$.

A word of caution. Not enough information was given in Task 69 to be absolutely sure what the next three numbers were. You needed to assume that there was some underlying numerical rule. If not, the next three numbers might be almost anything. Slightly ridiculous examples illustrate this: suppose the numbers came from buses arriving at a bus stop, lottery numbers or ages of children in a family. No sequence is unique unless there is an underlying rule.

Generalised arithmetic

Algebra is probably most often thought of as generalised arithmetic – 'you do to the letters what you usually do to the numbers'. But this only makes sense if you already know what it is that you do to numbers! You need be able to attend to how you do computations rather than just to what the answer is. It is not at all easy to describe in words what you do, but struggling to express it is important in the development of your mathematical thinking. This process takes considerable practice and experience, and so it is well worth working on at every opportunity.

Look at this:

$(3 \times 4 + 8) \div 5$

This expression can be seen in two ways:

▶ as a set of instructions for calculating;

▶ as a number, 4, the result of carrying out the calculation.

This dual aspect of an expression – as procedure and as answer – is central to algebraic thinking. This section concentrates on the first of them.

Task 70	Something plus something

$4 + 5 =$ $\qquad$ $5 + 4 =$

Notice that you get the same answer to both of the calculations shown. Does this always work? How might you express it more generally?

Comment

Letting F stand for 'First number', and S for 'Second number', you could express the generality illustrated by $4 + 5 = 5 + 4$ as $F + S = S + F$.

Here you need to shift your attention from what kinds of calculations you can do (like adding, subtracting, etc.), to what properties those calculations have. For example, $4 + 5$ equals $5 + 4$ not just because they both have the answer 9, but because it does not matter in which order you do the calculation. The underlying property is a rule of arithmetic, and also a rule for manipulating algebraic symbols.

Properties of operations

This section looks at the underlying properties of the operations of arithmetic. There are several different properties, which you probably often use without really thinking about them. Being aware of them will enable you to use them more consciously and effectively, as well as deepening your understanding of number.

Task 71	Mental tricks

Work these out mentally:

(a) $7 + 8 + 3 + 2$

(b) $5 \times 13 \times 2$

(c) $53 - 28 + 7 - 2$

(d) $7 + 95$

Think about how you did the calculations. Did you find any shortcuts? Can you see any quick ways of doing them now?

Comment

The answers do not matter, what is important here are the methods. The quick methods all involve carrying out the calculations in a different order to the way they are written. In (a) it is much quicker to work out $7 + 3$ and $8 + 2$ and then add the results. Similar strategies work in parts (b) and (c). In part (d) many people reverse the sum and start with 95 and add 7 to it (you possibly did not even notice yourself doing it). The methods for (a) and (d) work because it does not matter in what order you add numbers together, nor which additions you carry out first. That is also true for multiplication.

With these calculation shortcuts you make use of some of the properties of the number system. These properties all have formal names. Although you may need to be able to recognise the names, it is more important to have a grasp of what the properties are. In order to understand the significance of these properties they need to be separated.

Order. With multiplication and addition, the order does not matter. In the sum $7 + 95$, the answer comes out the same when the numbers are reversed to $95 + 7$. Similarly $7 \times 5 = 5 \times 7$.

An operation which can be carried out in any order is called commutative. As you will see, this property does not hold for subtraction or division.

Pairing. When you add $13 + 8 + 2$, it does not matter if you first add the 13 and 8 together and then add 2, or if you first add 8 and 2 to get l0 and then work out 13 add 10. This can be shown using brackets:

$$13 + 8 + 2 = (13 + 8) + 2$$

or

$$13 + 8 + 2 = 13 + (8 + 2)$$

Notice that the order of the numbers is the same, it is the pairing that changes. An operation in which the pairing does not matter is called associative.

These two properties are now discussed in more detail.

This is quite different from ordinary language where for example, 'dead butterfly collector' has two different meanings depending on which words are paired (a hyphen can be used to clarify).

The commutative property: order does not matter

In Task 71, $7 + 95$ was changed to $95 + 7$. This is possible for any type of number. The operations of addition and multiplication are commutative, written in mathematical shorthand:

$$a + b = b + a \text{ and } a \times b = b \times a$$

where a and b could be integers, fractions, or any other kind of number, or even an algebraic expression.

However, the order in which calculations are carried out does matter with other operations.

Task 72	Commutative

Are subtraction and division commutative? Try some examples (specialise).

Comment

Neither subtraction nor division are commutative: the order of the numbers matters. For example:

$$5 - 2 = 3 \text{ but } 2 - 5 = {}^-3$$
$$6 \div 3 = 2 \text{ but } 3 \div 6 = \frac{1}{2}$$

Notice that it is only necessary to have one counter-example of each to show that subtraction and division are not commutative.

The associative property: pairing does not matter

$$13 + 8 + 2 = (13 + 8) + 2 = 13 + (8 + 2)$$

Again, this holds for any type of number. The operation of addition is associative, in general form:

$$(a + b) + c = a + (b + c)$$

where a, b and c are *any* number.

Task 73	More association

Replace the symbol ∘ in 8 ∘ 4 ∘ 2 by ×, – and ÷ in turn. Pair off each in two different ways, using brackets, and see whether the answers are different.

Which of subtraction, multiplication and division are associative and which are not?

Comment

Multiplication is associative, but subtraction and division are not. For example:

$(8 - 4) - 2 = 4 - 2 = 2$ but $8 - (4 - 2) = 8 \times {}^-2 = 6$

so

$(8 - 4) - 2 \neq 8 - (4 - 2)$

$\neq$ is the symbol for 'is not equal to'.

Mixing addition and multiplication

The two properties discussed so far are sufficient to be able to change the order and pairings in any calculation involving just addition or just multiplication. Calculations which involve a mixture of addition and multiplication often make use of another property, the distributive property. This is explained through looking at a method of long

Analysing a method	Task 74

multiplication.

Work through the multiplication of 37 by 19 using your own preferred written method and then list the individual calculations of which it comprises (even if you do some of them in your head).

Comment

There are many ways of doing the calculation, but one common method of 'long multiplication' is analysed below (this may be different to the way you 'see' it, so be prepared to work through it slowly):

```
   37
   19    Think of 19 as (10 + 9)
  370    (10 × 7) + (10 × 30)
  333    (9 × 7) + (9 × 30)
  703    (10 × 37) + (9 × 37)
```

It is perhaps not surprising that few children understand this method and most have to practise it many times before being able do it.

Writing this method another way:

$37 \times 19 = 37 \times (10 + 9) = (37 \times 10) + (37 \times 9)$

Visually, considering the numbers as arrays of dots, the method can be illustrated as follows:

This property is known as the distributive law of multiplication over addition. Written out in general form it is:

$a(b + c) = (a \times b) + (a \times c)$

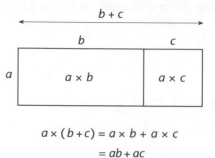

$$a \times (b+c) = a \times b + a \times c$$
$$= ab + ac$$

which can be represented by a similar diagram.

This property is used for multiplying out algebraic expressions as well as numbers, so:

$$3(x + y) = 3x + 3y$$

There is an equivalent property for subtraction:

$$a(b - c) = (a \times b) - (a \times c)$$
$$= ab - ac$$

Task 75	Links

What links do you see between the notions of expressing generality in patterns and generalised arithmetic? Try thinking about what is the same and what is different. (You may find this difficult; but the process of trying to think about both notions of algebra will help you to reflect on your learning so far.)

Comment

When asked this question, one learner came up with the following statement.

> In both, letters are used to represent numbers. In expressing generality, letters are combined to make a pattern stand out, to make a relationship obvious so it can be used as a rule for calculating outputs from inputs. In generalised arithmetic the letters are used to highlight a statement that is always true whatever kind of number or expression the letters represent.

Equations – finding the unknown

Think back to a time in the past when you encountered equations (or a particular equation), and recall any memories that you have. This may involve thinking back a number of years to when you were taught equations at school or recalling any moment in your life where the idea of an equation was relevant.

You may find that the following sorts of things come to mind.

- Equations are things you have to solve to find x.

- You have to balance the left- and right-hand sides.

- Whatever you do to one side, you must do to the other.

- You have to find the missing number.

- Change the side, change the sign.

- Find the value of x.

- There are simultaneous equations that have both x and y.

Most of these statements involve equations as things to be acted upon and on the methods or techniques that are often taught. This section revisits the topic of equations and will try to give you a perspective on equations which is not simply about methods for solving them.

The most usual methods taught in schools to solve equations are based on algebra. This is mainly because, when such methods are possible, they give exact answers. This section concentrates on that use of algebra.

In science and engineering and other areas where mathematics is used frequently, many equations are solved by using graphs or by putting in numerical values.

What is an equation? | Task 76

Look through this list of statements and decide which ones you would consider to be equations and which ones you would not.

$7 + 3 = 10$	$2x - 1 = 29$	$V = IR$
$(y - 3)(y + 4)$	$2x + 3 = x + 1$	$ax + by + c = 0$
$x + y = 10$	$4a = a + a + a + a$	$x = 5$

Comment

There is no single 'right' definition of an equation; but all equations have an equals sign and most involve some algebraic expression. People disagree, for instance, about whether a letter has to be present or whether an equation can consist only of letters, as in the formula $V = IR$ (Ohm's law). $(y - 3)(y + 4)$ is an algebraic expression, but is not an equation since there is no equals sign.

Mary Boole (1832–1916) was an influential mathematics teacher and educator. Her writings are full of wise observations which are remarkably modern in their perceptiveness and expression. Possibly her most famous observation is as follows.

When people had only arithmetic and not algebra, they found out a surprising amount of things about numbers and quantities. But there remained problems which they very much needed to solve and could not. They had to guess the answer; and, of course, they usually guessed wrong […] At last (at least I should suppose this is what happened) some man, or perhaps some woman, suddenly said: 'How stupid we've all been! We have been dealing logically with all the facts we knew about this problem, except the most important fact of all, the fact of our own ignorance. Let us include that among the facts we have to be logical about, and see where we get to then. In this problem besides the numbers which we do know, there is one we do not know. Instead of guessing whether we are to call it none, or seven, or a hundred and twenty, or a thousand and fifty, let us agree to call it x, and let us always remember that x stands for the Unknown. Let us write x in among all our other numbers, and deal logically with it according to exactly the same laws as we deal with six or nine or a hundred or a thousand.'   (Tahta 1972)

Mary's husband, George, is known for Boolean algebra: the logic used by computers.

Mary Boole's notion of acknowledging ignorance comes into its own in tasks like the following, the kind of problems which many people associate with algebra.

Think of a number

Look at these 'think of a number' problems.

▶ I have a number in mind. I double it, add 3 and the answer is 131. What's my number?

▶ I have a number in my mind. I subtract 1 and multiply by 3, then subtract 7 and the answer is 8. What's my number?

These questions correspond to equations, the first to $2x + 3 = 131$, the second to $3(x - 1) - 7 = 8$. The fact that word puzzles like these can be written as equations gives a way of thinking about equations. When these equations are treated like number problems, you can use an informal method of solving them. This method may be called 'working backwards' or 'undoing'. For example, on the first of the problems:

If the number has been doubled and then 3 added to give a result of 131, then before the 3 was added, it had to be 128 (3 less than 131).

So, a number has been doubled to give 128, therefore the original number is 64 (half of 128).

A diagram, such as the one below, perhaps shows more clearly the 'undoing' nature of this method.

Doing			Undoing		
A number	x		The number	64	
Double it	$2x$		Halve it	$128 \div 2$	
Add three	$2x + 3$		Subtract 3	$131 - 3$	
Answer	$2x + 3 = 131$		Answer	131	

To use 'think of a number' problems as a means of solving equations you need to be able to translate between the words and the equation. You need to be able to carry out this translating both ways. Here is the translation of the second 'think of a number' problem:

Doing		
A number	x
Subtract 1	$x - 1$
Multiply by 3	$3(x + 1)$
Subtract 7	$3(x + 1) - 7$
Answer 8	$3(x + 1) - 7 = 8$

Note the use of brackets to show the order of operations (brackets first).

Undoing Task 77

Take the second 'think of a number' problem above and find the solution by working backwards 'undoing' each operation in turn.

Comment

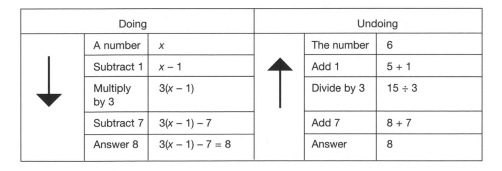

Doing			Undoing		
A number	x		The number	6	
Subtract 1	$x - 1$		Add 1	$5 + 1$	
Multiply by 3	$3(x - 1)$		Divide by 3	$15 \div 3$	
Subtract 7	$3(x - 1) - 7$		Add 7	$8 + 7$	
Answer 8	$3(x - 1) - 7 = 8$		Answer	8	

Translating Task 78

1 Translate these equations and number problems into the other form.

(a)   I am thinking of a number. I subtract 5, multiply by 2, add 4 and the answer is 12. What is my number?

(b)   I am thinking of a number. I add 7, multiply by 2, subtract 10 and finally divide by 5. The result is 2. What was my original number?

(c) $2x + 4 = 12$

(d) $2\left(\frac{x}{3} - 5\right) + 4 = 12$

2   Find 'the number' using the 'undoing' method.

Comment

1   The answers to the translation task are:

(a) $2(x - 5) + 4 = 12$

(b) $\frac{2(x + 7) - 10}{5} = 2$

(c)   I am thinking of a number. I multiply by 2, add 4 and the answer is 12. What is my number?

(d)   I am thinking of a number. I divide by 3, subtract 5, multiply by 2, add 4 and the answer is 12. What is my number?

2   (a) 9;

(b) 3;

(c) 4;

(d) 27.

This concerns the topic often called simultaneous equations.

Pairs of equations

When you were asked to think about what an equation is, one of the expressions given was:

$x + y = 10$

This has an equal sign and algebraic symbols, but differs from the equations just considered because it has two unknowns and expresses a relationship between them. It could be translated into a 'think of a number' problem:

I'm thinking of two numbers which add to 10.

There is no single 'solution' to this equation, but infinitely many pairs of numbers that fit. Here are some of them:

$x = 3, y = 7$
$x = 9, y = 1$
$x = {}^-3, y = 13$
$x = 1.6, y = 8.4$
$x = 110, y = {}^-100$

But if a second clue is given, for example:

the two numbers also differ by 4. Translated into an algebraic equation, this is: $x - y = 4$. Then there is only one pair of numbers that can satisfy both clues.

Two clues	Task 79

(a) Find the numbers which fit both of the two clues. I'm thinking of two numbers which add to 10. The two numbers also differ by 4.

(b) What are the two numbers if they differ by 6 instead of by 4? by 2? by 8? by 12? by 7? Trying all of these should give you a sense of how the values of the two numbers change as the condition alters. Make up some more if you are still not confident.

(c) Try some others.

   (i) I'm thinking of two numbers which add to 12. The two numbers also differ by 4.

   (ii) I'm thinking of two numbers which add to 100. The two numbers also differ by 36.

(d) Make up similar problems for yourself.

Remember that being able to make up suitable examples is a good way of assessing how much you understand.

Comment

Such questions as these are self-checking. If the two numbers fit the initial conditions, then they must be the correct values. What is important here is that you develop some awareness of how the numbers depend on the conditions and develop some informal methods of finding the numbers.

You might wonder whether there is any value in expressing such problems in algebra rather than words. Algebra is briefer, but perhaps not as easy to understand. There is an advantage in symbols as the following shows.

Consider these two clues.

I'm thinking of two numbers which add to 8.

I double the first number and add the second to get 14.

Expressed in symbols these clues are:

$$x + y = 8$$
$$2x + y = 14$$

Looking at the left-hand sides of these equations notice that the bottom equation has an extra x. Logically, this x must be equal to the increase on the right-hand side, $6 = (14 - 8)$. So $x = 6$ and, because x and y add to 8, $y = 2$.

Notice what was involved here. You need to think about what the equations *mean*, and to be able to move between the symbols and numbers.

Task 80	Pairs of equations

Find the solutions to the following pairs of equations.

(a) $\begin{aligned} 4x + y &= 44 \\ x + y &= 20 \end{aligned}$

(b) $\begin{aligned} 4x + 3y &= 247 \\ 4x - y &= 83 \end{aligned}$

(c) $\begin{aligned} 6x + y &= 90 \\ 3x - y &= 9 \end{aligned}$

Comment

The answers are self-checking (the numbers must fit *both* equations) so you should know whether you have the correct solutions. If you were 'stuck' then there are some hints below.

In part (a) comparison gives $3x = 24$, and for (b) $4y = 164$. But, in part (c), when you compare the two equations, you get another equation with both x and y in it, $3x + 2y = 81$. This seems to leave you no better off, but if you then compare this with the second of the equations, you will be able to get the value for y.

Formulas

There has been a shift over the years in the plural for formula. In older books it was written 'formulæ', then 'formulae' became standard, and now 'formulas' is the most used plural.

Formulas are used a great deal outside of mathematics, often as a set of instructions for calculating. They mostly relate to some specific relationship, rather than being an abstract equation. Even so, they are really just a particular kind of equation and so can be used and manipulated in the same way as equations.

These are some formulas that you may have met.

The area A of a triangle (where b = base, h = height):

$$A = \tfrac{1}{2} bh.$$

Changing Fahrenheit (°F) temperatures into Celsius (°C):

$$C = \tfrac{5}{9} (F - 32).$$

Connecting distance, time and speed:

$$\text{speed} = \tfrac{\text{distance}}{\text{time}}.$$

The circumference C of a circle (where r = radius):

$C = 2\pi r$.

Einstein's equation (e = energy, m = mass, c is the speed of light):

$e = mc^2$.

One of the formulas above is for converting temperatures in degrees Fahrenheit to degrees Celsius. Written in words it says:

To get the Celsius temperature, take the Fahrenheit temperature and subtract 32; multiply the result by 5 and divide by 9 (or, otherwise, multiply by $\frac{5}{9}$).

Words for formulas	Task 81

Write each of the formulas above in words, in a form of instructions for carrying out a calculation.

Comment

Suitable forms are as follows (yours may differ slightly).

Area of a triangle: take the length of the base, multiply it by the height and divide by 2.

Speed: divide distance by time

The circumference of a circle: multiply the radius by pi and then by 2.

Energy: multiply the speed of light by itself and then by the mass.

Substituting in formulas

Putting numbers in formulas is straightforward if the formula is designed to give you exactly the information you want. Sometimes the formula is arranged 'the wrong way'. For example, you may want to convert from °C to °F but the formula

$C = \frac{5}{9}(F - 32)$

converts the other way.

Formulas usually refer to quantities, so care has to be taken with the units of measure particularly with compound measures, such as mph.

Use the formulas above to find these values:

(a) the area of a triangle with base 5 cm and height 12 cm;

(b) the Celsius temperature corresponding to 80 °F;

(c) the distance covered at a speed of 43 km/hour for 1.3 hours;

(d) the height of a triangle, whose base is 3.2 cm and whose area is 14.7 cm².

Comment

The answers to these are:

(a) 30 cm²;

(b) 26.7 °C;

(c) 55.9 km;

(d) 9.19 cm.

(The temperature and height are given to 3 significant figures.)

While the first two of these involve straightforward substitution into the formulas, the others are more tricky, since the formula in each case is written 'the wrong way round'.

There are two ways of dealing with this difficulty in substituting. The first method is simply to put the numbers in the formula and then see what you have to do to find the answer. So, with the part (d) above, putting in the numbers gives:

$$14.7 = \tfrac{1}{2} \times 3.2 \times h$$

This simplifies to $14.7 = 1.6h$, and so h can then be found as $14.7 \div 1.6$.

This method often works quite well, but if you have several calculations to carry out the wrong way round, it is often quicker to rearrange the formula, and use the new one. There are various methods for rearranging formulas, but the one you are most likely to need is the 'undoing' method, which was used with equations.

As an example, look again at the formula for converting temperatures in degrees Fahrenheit to degrees Celsius:

$$C = \tfrac{5}{9} \ (F - 32)$$

Translating this as an instruction for calculating a Fahrenheit temperature to its Celsius equivalent can be thought of as a 'doing'. To get the formula the other way round that doing needs to be converted to an 'undoing'.

Doing			Undoing		
Temperature in Fahrenheit	F		Formula for Celsius to Fahrenheit	$F = \frac{9}{5}(C + 32)$	
Subtract 32	$F - 32$		Add 32	$\frac{9}{5}C + 32$	
Multiply by 5	$5(F - 32)$		Divide by 5	$\frac{9}{5}C$	
Divide by 9	$\frac{5}{9}(F - 32)$		Multiply by 9	$9C$	
Formula for Fahrenheit to Celsius	$C = \frac{5}{9}(F - 32)$		Temperature in Centigrade	C	

The important feature to notice in producing the diagram is that you need to start with the symbol that you wish to make the 'subject' of the formula. In this case there were only the two symbols C and F, but in the formula for the area of a triangle:

$$A = \frac{1}{2} bh$$

there are three symbols, any of which could become the 'subject'.

Rearrange the following formulas using the 'doing and undoing' method.

(a) The area of a triangle, $A = \frac{1}{2} bh$, to give a formula for the height.

(b) Speed $= \frac{\text{distance}}{\text{time}}$ to give a formula for:

    (i) distance and (ii) time.

(c) The circumference of a circle, $C = 2\pi r$, to give a formula for the radius.

(d) Einstein's equation, $e = mc^2$, to give a formula for c, the speed of light.

Comment

The answers are:

(a) $h = \frac{2A}{b}$

(b) (i) distance = speed × time   (ii) time $= \frac{\text{distance}}{\text{speed}}$

(c) $r = \frac{C}{2\pi}$ (d) $c = \sqrt{\frac{e}{m}}$ (remember square root 'undoes' squaring).

Picturing functions

Several of the formulas you have met so far concern the relationship between two quantities. For example:

The point of this is to enable you to tell at a glance which part of the function formula is being referred to.

The formula $C = \frac{5}{9}(F - 32)$ for converting degrees Fahrenheit to degrees Celsius shows a relationship between C and F. For any value of F there will be a corresponding value of C.

In the brick and picture example at the beginning of this chapter, the general formula $b = 2p - 1$ shows the relationship between b for the number of bricks and p for the picture number.

Relationships like these between two quantities are called functions. The formulas can be thought of as 'machines' which enable you to find the values corresponding to any number input. The formulas are a particularly useful way of representing a function when you want to find values, but do not reveal all the aspects of the relationship clearly. Functions can also be represented by tables and graphs, which emphasise different features and allow you to see other properties of the relationship.

In this section the connection between formulas, tables and graphs will be explored, including the use of graphs to solve equations. To keep matters simple, all of the functions will be written in a standard form using x and y. So, for example, the Fahrenheit and Celsius function will be written as:

$$y = \frac{5}{9}(x - 32)$$

and the brick picture function as:

$$y = 2x - 1.$$

Tables for functions

Tables are useful to get a feel for the values involved in a function and for drawing a graph if you need to do it by hand. Take the function $y = 3x + 1$. Values of this function can be shown in a table:

x	0	1	2	3	4	5	6 ...
$y = 3x + 1$	1	4	7	10	13	16	19 ...

Task 84	Looking across and down

Look along the y row of the table. Write down what you notice. Now look down each column to see the $3x + 1$ pattern.

Comment

The top row increases by one each time; the bottom row increases by 3. Or, put another way, there is a difference of 3 between adjacent numbers in the bottom row.

Reading down the columns in the table, the numbers can be written as ordered pairs (x, y):

(0, 1), (1, 4), (2, 7), (3, 10), (4, 13), ...

In each ordered pair, the second number is always 3 × (the first number) + 1.

These ordered pairs can then be plotted as points on a graph. The first value (the x value) is always on the horizontal axis.

Plotting a graph	Task 85

On the graph axes shown below, the first two ordered pairs from the table have been plotted. On the same axes plot the remaining pairs.

Write down what you notice.

Recall that each point is plotted by going horizontally first and then vertically.

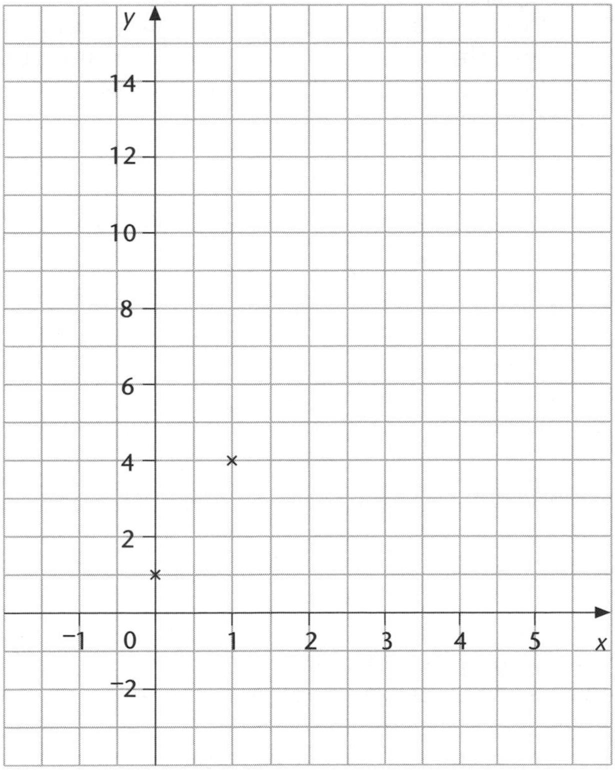

Comment

The points lie in a straight line. (If they are not in a straight line, check the plotting of each point. Notice that the scales are different on the x- and y-axes.)

This is a way of seeing that there is a pattern or relationship – in this case because the points are in a straight line it is called a linear relationship. The next 'higher' point can be generated by moving 1 right and up 3.

Of course, only some of the possible values were chosen for x – the positive whole number values. Since any decimal value or negative value could be chosen, the points on the graph are only a selection. All of the points are represented by the straight line through the plotted points. Draw in the line and extend it to the edges of the diagram.

Plotting graphs

This method of representing a function on a graph allows you to see features that may not be obvious from the formula or table (for example, in the case above, that the points lie on a straight line). This section will examine features of functions that show up on their graphs. The functions studied will all be linear functions, which produce straight line graphs.

You may prefer to use a graphics calculator or computer plotting application for the tasks in this section.

To discover the features of linear functions, you need to explore them systematically. The graph plotted above was of the function $y = 3x + 1$. A useful procedure is to vary the numbers in the formula and look at what happens to the graph. Since there are two numbers (3 and 1) it is better to vary only one of them at a time. In the next task it is the '1' that is varied.

Task 86	Drawing lines

Create the tables for the functions:

$$y = 3x + 4, \quad y = 3x - 2, \quad y = 3x, \quad y = 3x - 1$$

On the same diagram as you used in Task 85, draw the graphs of these functions.

What do you notice about the lines? Try to generalise your observations.

Comment

The lines are all parallel, but cut the axes at different points. You may have noticed a connection between the numbers that are being varied and the points at which they cut the y-axis. If not, look carefully, and if necessary plot some more functions of the same kind.

The varying number indicates where the graph will cut the y-axis. The technical word for this is the y-intercept.

The other number to be varied in the formula $y = 3x + 1$ is the 3.

Create the tables for the functions:

$$y = 2x - 1, \quad y = 5x - 1, \quad y = x - 1, \quad y = {}^-2x - 1, \quad y = {}^-3x - 1$$

Use axes for x from $^-4$ to 4, and y from $^-5$ to 15 to draw the graphs of these functions on a single diagram.

What do you notice about the lines? Try to generalise your observations.

Comment

The lines all pass through the same point on the y-axis (y = $^-1$, because they all have $^-1$ as the 'other number', the y-intercept). But they vary in steepness, with two of them sloping down from left to right. You may have noticed that the steeper lines have the bigger numbers, and that the two lines sloping down from left to right have negative numbers. There is a more precise connection between the numbers and the steepness. See if you can find this connection, if necessary plotting some more functions of the same kind.

The steepness of a line is given by its gradient. This is found by seeing how much the line rises for a 'run' of 1 across.

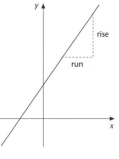

Notice that you need to take care with the scales here. You must take the actual x and y values – you cannot just count the spaces. The gradient in each of the lines is the number multiplying the x (this is called the coefficient of x).

The results of these last two tasks enable you to draw the graph of any linear function without having to create a table. The general form of the linear function is:

$$y = mx + c.$$

The value of m gives the gradient of the line, and the value of c gives the point on which it crosses the y-axis.

Identify which lines on the graph overleaf belong with which equation.

$$y = 2x + 3 \quad y = x + 2 \quad y = 2x - 3 \quad y = {}^-3x + 3$$

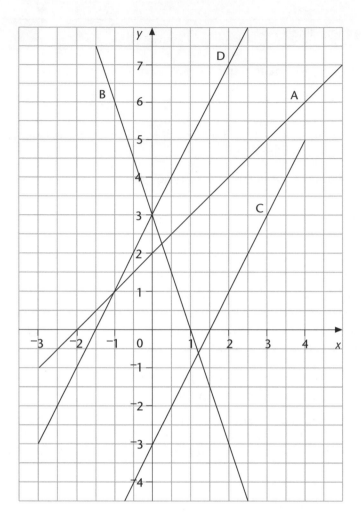

Comment

A is $y = x + 2$, B is $y = {}^{-}3x + 3$, C is $y = 2x - 3$ and D is $y = 2x + 3$.

Solving equations with graphs

Being able to plot graphs gives another method for solving equations. Look at the graphs in Task 88. Graphs A and D cross at the point ($^{-}$1, 1). This means that:

$x = {}^{-}1, y = 1$

fits both the equations:

$y = x + 2$ and $y = 2x + 3$.

You can easily check this by substituting the numbers.

Where there is a pair of equations like these, they can be solved by drawing graphs and finding the intersection point. This is an alternative to the algebraic method described earlier.

Use the graphs in Task 88 to solve these pairs of equations.

(a) $y = 2x + 3$ and $y = {}^-3x + 3$

(b) $y = 2x - 3$ and $y = {}^-3x + 3$

Comment

The solution to (a) is $x = 0$, $y = 3$; to (b) it is $x = 1.2$, $y = {}^-0.6$.

The answer to part (b) shows one of the problems of using graphs to solve equations: it is very difficult to get an exact answer. However, if an approximate answer is all that is needed, then plotting graphs can be a useful alternative to using algebraic methods (especially when a graphics calculator or a computer is available).

Inequalities

So far you have been dealing with equations and using the equals sign. In everyday life you are more likely to meet situations which have a range of solutions and use phrases such as 'more than' or 'fewer than' or their equivalent. These expression are called 'inequalities' and the symbols used for their shorthand are:

> < meaning 'fewer than' or 'less than' or 'smaller than', as in $3 < 7$ (smaller < larger];
> ≤, meaning 'less than or equal to';
> >, meaning 'greater than', 'more than', 'larger than', as in $7 > 3$ larger > smaller;
> ≥, meaning 'greater than or equal to'.

Musicians use similar symbols: an elongated < for crescendo (quiet to loud) and > for diminuendo (from loud to quiet).

When you buy car insurance there are several variables to consider, such as the type of car that is to be insured, the place where it will be kept and details of the driver including age. The way ages are grouped or categorised is not always clear. For example a 'young driver' could be described as being aged 17 to 24. How do you interpret this? If you have had your twenty-fourth birthday recently, you may wonder whether this includes you or not. If you know that the next group is listed as 25 to 29 then this may help, but in mathematics, sets need to be defined precisely. This can be done in symbols or diagrams.

For example 'aged 17 to 24' includes all ages from 17 (including 17 exactly) to all those who are 24 but not yet 25:

> $17 \le$ age of driver < 25

> or if the age is called a, then: $17 \le a < 25$.

Pictures are also used for inequalities, with a filled circle to show that the value can be included and an empty circle to show it cannot. For example:

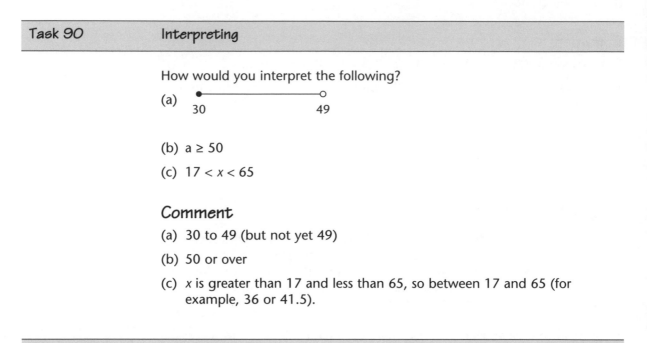

17   25

| Task 90 | Interpreting |

How would you interpret the following?

(a)
30   49

(b) $a \geq 50$

(c) $17 < x < 65$

Comment

(a) 30 to 49 (but not yet 49)

(b) 50 or over

(c) x is greater than 17 and less than 65, so between 17 and 65 (for example, 36 or 41.5).

| Task 91 | Reflection |

Think back over the whole of this chapter. Try to answer the question 'Where is the algebra?'.

Comment

Your list may include some of the following:

▶ drawing pictures;

▶ counting specialised examples;

▶ predicting the next;

▶ constructing a table;

▶ working out a rule;

▶ stating the properties of arithmetic;

▶ expressing rules or relationships in actions, words, and symbols (using expressions, equations, or functions);

▶ drawing a graph.

In some sense the algebra is in the mathematical thinking – the pictures, words and symbols are records of that thinking. They are a means of communicating your thinking to yourself and, with agreed ways of recording, to other people.

Summary

This chapter has introduced you to different, but connected aspects of Algebra. It has covered:

◗ finding and using pattern;

◗ generalised arithmetic;

◗ finding the as yet unknown;

◗ using formulas;

◗ picturing functions;

◗ inequalities.

There has been an emphasis on algebraic thinking through expressing the same thing in different forms and 'doing and undoing'.

Further study

Gattegno, C. (1977) *What We Owe Children*, Routledge and Kegan Paul.

Mason, J. with Graham, A. and Johnston-Wilder, S. (2005) *Developing Thinking in Algebra*, Paul Chapman Publishing.

Mason, J., Graham, A., Pimm, D. and Gower, N. (1985) *Routes to/Roots of Algebra*, The Open University.

Tahta, D. (ed.) (1972) *A Boolean Anthology: Selected Writings of Mary Boole on Mathematical Education*, ATM.

6 Geometry

Introduction

Although it is now often called 'shape and space', geometry is the original term for the study of relationships between points, lines, circles, planes and other 2D and 3D objects. Geometry has a very long history, arising from the practical measurement of land in the Nile delta in ancient Egypt and the geometry as developed by the Greeks around 500 BC. Greek geometry did not involve actual measuring, and was the study of properties of shape and space that has developed into the area of mathematics known as geometry today. There are two central aspects to geometry dealt with in this section: relationships and generality.

The origins of the word geometry lie in measuring (metry) the earth (geo).

Lengths, angles, areas and volumes are commonly thought of as involving measurement. But there are many relationships between lengths or areas that do not depend upon measuring. For example, the two diagonals of a rectangle must be equal in length, even though what this length is may not be known; or, if a triangle is equilateral (all three sides are equal), then all three angles must also be equal. Rulers or protractors are not needed to deduce those results. Geometry is about establishing such relationships, usually by thinking and reasoning about diagrams. Of course, geometrical results are often very useful in practical measuring.

Practical measurement is dealt with in Chapter 3.

Geometry, like all of mathematics, is pervaded by generalising. What is important is not a specific triangle or a particular circle, but properties of *all* circles, *all* rectangles, *all* triangles. The features of shapes such as lengths, area and volume are frequently expressed in formulas, which use algebra. Algebra is used to express generality when quantities are involved, while geometry is the expression of generality when relationships between points, lines, circles, etc. are involved.

See Chapter 5 for other aspects of generalising.

Geometry is an excellent domain for working on developing powers of mental imagery, which will then support both mental mathematics and writing. Consequently, you are often asked to imagine some geometrical objects moving and to visualise relationships between parts of a figure. You may find this unfamiliar at first, but once you become experienced you will find it a powerful way of relating geometric properties and understanding why various results are true. To capture your imaginings you will often need to draw a diagram as a typical snapshot. There are many drawn diagrams in this section and it is helpful to carry out the reverse process with them: seeing each diagram as a single frame from some mental film.

If you have access to a computer, you may be able to use a dynamic geometry package which can be very like producing a film on the computer screen that corresponds to your mental one; but, of course, it is much easier to see what is happening.

Often, when referring to parts of a diagram, it is necessary to give them labels. The simplest way might be to colour the lines, so reference could be made to 'the red line' or 'the green circle', but that is not possible in this book. So the device of labelling points *A*, *B*, *C*, … and lines as AB, BC, … or *a*, *b*, *c*, … and using combinations of them such a 'angle *ABC*' will be used. It is always rather laborious to read, but unfortunately is unavoidable.

Colouring is possible with dynamic geometry software.

This chapter is in four sections:

▶ *basic ideas of shape and space* – points, lines and angles, constructions, and transformations of shapes;

▶ *properties of 2D shapes* – concentrating on quadrilaterals;

▶ *lengths and areas in two dimensions* – length and area relationships for shapes, including Pythagoras' theorem;

▶ *geometry in three dimensions* – some types of 3D shapes and their properties including volumes and areas.

Basic ideas of shape and space

Lines and angles

This section looks at the most basic features of geometry: lines and angles. It considers types of angles, and the properties of angles formed by parallel lines and by triangles.

Types of angles
The diagram shows a fixed arm and a rotating arm (with the arrow), which have an angle formed between them. Imagine the moving arm starting on top of the fixed one and then rotating in the direction of the arrow. Focus on the size of the marked angle. At first the angle is quite sharp, but becoming less so. It becomes a right angle, and then much blunter until the two lines form a straight line. It then starts to 'turn back upon itself' (it is bigger than the other angle formed by the two lines), passes through a three-quarter turn and then, as the arm gets back to the start, lies on top of the fixed arm again. Most of these angles have names.

▶ When the angle is sharp (still less than a right angle) it is called acute.

▶ When the arm has rotated through one-quarter of a full turn the angle is called a right angle. The two lines are said to be perpendicular.

▶ When the angle is between a right angle and a straight line, the angle is called obtuse (compare 'thick').

▶ When the angle is greater than a straight line and less than a full turn, it is called reflex. (There is no special word for an angle between a three-quarter turn and a full turn.)

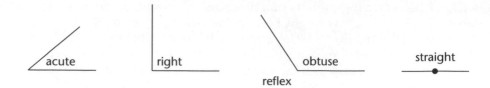

Sometimes it is necessary to refer to a turn which involves more than one full revolution, so it is possible to have angles of arbitrarily large size.

Imagine the arm rotating once more, but this time focus on the other angle between the lines. You should see that it behaves in the opposite way to the marked angle: it starts as a reflex angle and decreases. There is a moment when the two lines form a straight line and both angles are equal; then this other angle becomes an obtuse angle, then a right angle, then acute and finally goes to zero.

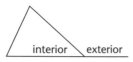

Any pair of angles that make a right angle are called complementary (even when they are not next to each other). Similarly for supplementary.

Because there are two angles formed by two lines meeting at a point, often there is a need to distinguish between them, particularly when referring to angles in shapes. An angle is called interior if it is 'inside' the triangle or other polygon. The angle between an edge extended and an adjacent edge is an exterior angle.

With the rotating arm, you were able to focus on the marked angle and its 'opposite' angle making a full turn. Instead of thinking of the opposite in a full turn you can also think of opposite angles formed between a pair of lines. In the diagram, the rotating arm now only moves between the two fixed lines. As the arm rotates, the marked angle increases and the opposite angle decreases. When the fixed lines are at right angles the angle and its opposite are called complementary angles. When the fixed lines form a straight line the two angles are called supplementary angles.

Task 92	Angles arising from parallel lines

Imagine a straight line on a flat surface. Move it about in your mind so as to get a sense of the freedom you have. Bring it to rest. Make a copy of it and slide that copy around so that it never alters direction, never rotates. Bring it back on top of its original line and hold it still.

Create a third line cutting the first line at an angle (it will also cut the copy). Pay attention to the angles this new line makes with the original line (perhaps even mark one of those angles mentally). Are any of the angles the same size? Again slide the copy. There are now angles between the new line and the copy. How do those angles change as the copy is slid about?

Comment

You should see that the sizes of the angles do not change even though their positions do. There are many equal pairs of angles in the diagram.

When any two straight lines cut, the angles opposite each other are equal (they are called opposite angles or, sometimes, 'vertically opposite' angles – although they need not be vertical). This is shown by each pair having the same letter, such as $a = a'$. Because the angles stay the same when the copy is slid about, each of the four angles between the copy and the third line is the same as the corresponding one of the original four angles. Hence the name for such equal pairs – corresponding angles.

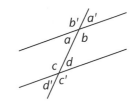

Knowing that opposite angles are equal and corresponding angles are equal, it is quite easy to deduce that other pairs are equal. The equal pair a and d, and the pair c and b are known as alternate or Z-angles (because they lie in a Z-shape). Perhaps surprisingly, there is no name for the equal pair a' and d' and the pair c' and b'.

Locating equal angles	Task 93

In the diagram, lines parallel to the same direction are marked by the same kind of arrows. All the marked angles are equal, either because they are opposite angles or because of the effect of parallel lines. Starting with the heavily marked angle a, you can deduce that any other marked angle is equal to it by following a chain of other equal angles that are each opposite or corresponding or alternate to the previous one. For example, to show that h is equal to a:

$a = c$ (corresponding) $\rightarrow$ $c = d$ (opposite) $\rightarrow$
$d = f$ (corresponding) $\rightarrow$ $f = h$ (corresponding)

(a) There are other chains that could be made between a and h. Produce two of them.

(b) Find chains between a and j and a chain that takes you back by a different route from j to a.

(c) The diagram below is made up of lines parallel to one of two directions. Mark all the angles you can find which are equal to the marked angle.

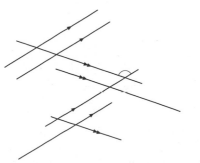

Knowing these results about angles between parallel lines it is possible to deduce other results, including the famous one that the angles of a triangle add up to 180°.

Angles in a triangle
Look at the figure below.

Hint: the two parts of angle *d* are each equal to one of the angles *a* and *b*.

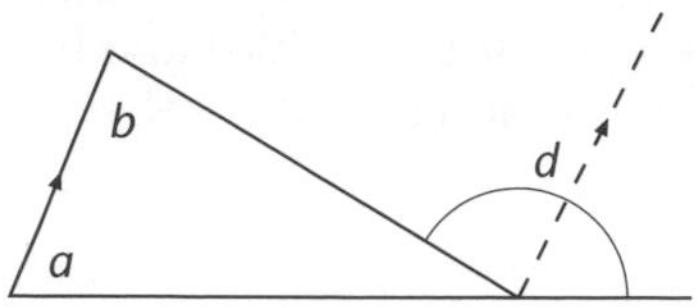

Using the properties of parallel lines it is possible to show that the angle *d*, an exterior angle of the triangle, is the sum of the angles *a* and *b*.

This result is often expressed as:

> the exterior angle of a triangle is equal to the sum of the two interior opposite angles.

This is quite a simple result – but not one that would be obvious just by looking at triangles. It has been produced by reasoning about the properties of angles and parallel lines.

The most famous result about angles in triangles is:

> the sum of the (interior) angles of a (planar) triangle is 180°.

What do the different words in this statement contribute? For example, *sum* tells you what operation to perform; *angle* indicates what to attend to; *triangle* provides the context; and 180° tells you what the answer is. But the most easily overlooked word is a, because it hides the generality. The statement applies to *every and all* triangles (which lie in a plane). Not just one or two triangles; not just some triangles drawn in a book; but each and every triangle no matter when or where drawn or imagined, or by whom.

Of course, the statement is theoretical: it applies to pure triangles. If you try to measure the angles of a particular triangle then you run into practical problems involving the thickness of lines, the imprecision of a protractor, and so on. Although this result is often given as the 'the angles of a triangle add up to 180°', the total angle need not be described as 180° (i.e., in degrees, as if it was being measured). It could be described as 'half a complete turn', 'two right angles', or that the three angles 'fit together to make a straight line'. None of these involve actual measuring.

How can it be known that the statement about the sum of the interior angles of a triangle is always true? Below are two different proofs (chains of reasoning): each sheds particular light on the result.

Proof 1

It has been shown below that the exterior angle of a triangle is the sum of the two interior opposite ones. The third angle of the triangle forms a 'straight angle of 180°' with this exterior angle.

Further comments on the role of proof in mathematics can be found in Chapter 8.

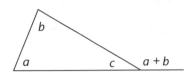

Proof 2

Consider any triangle. Imagine a tiny pencil with the blunt end at a vertex and pointing along one edge of the triangle so that it would traverse the triangle in a clockwise direction. Slide the pencil along the edge until the sharp end is at the next vertex. Rotate the pencil about that vertex corresponding to the interior angle of the triangle until it coincides with the next edge. Repeat the slide and rotation until the pencil is back where it started (but pointing in the opposite direction!). Through what total angle has the pencil rotated? What then is the sum of the angles of the triangle?

Tessellating triangles
Look at the diagram below.

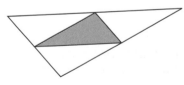

Through every vertex of the shaded triangle, a line is drawn parallel to the opposite side. Three more triangles are produced. By the properties of angles and parallel lines it is possible to show that each of these triangles has its three angles the same as the original triangle. In fact, the three triangles are identical (congruent) to the original triangle, but rotated.

There was nothing special about the triangle used here. All triangles tile the plane.

The procedure is repeated by drawing lines through the vertices of the new triangle parallel to each of the opposite sides, and this repeated again, and again, and so on. The whole plane can be covered in this way.

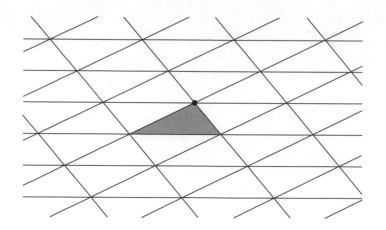

The diagram above shows part of the plane covered in a tiling of triangles.

(a) Look at the diagram in different ways.

  (i)   See it as versions of the original triangle. Pick out those triangles that are in the same position as the original triangle.

  (ii) See it made up of parallelograms tiling the plane.

  (iii) See it as a different set of parallelograms tiling the plane.

  (iv) See it as three sets of parallel lines.

(b) Imagine the marked point moving along the horizontal line, dragging the two other sides of the original triangle with it – and, of course, all of the other lines parallel to each of them. Can you make a diagram consisting of rectangles (each with one diagonal)? Can you make the diagram be a different set of rectangles?

This diagram will be used again in the section on transformations.

Comment

The purpose of this task is to assist you in developing your ability to become flexible in your mental imagery and to see shapes embedded in other shapes.

Constructions

There are many constructions used to create different figures but these cannot be dealt with in detail here. This section will give you a way of thinking about constructions that you can use in further work.

Using tools such as rulers, compasses and set-squares to construct geometrical diagrams may seem rather pointless when you can use squared paper, or even a computer. The purpose of thinking about such constructions is not so much to give you methods of drawing (although they do that) as to help you see how shapes can be built up by a sequence of constructions, with each step depending on the previous ones, and to see what are the minimal tools you need for any construction.

Suppose, for example, that you have only an unmarked set-square (a right-angled triangle), so that you can draw a line joining two points and you can draw a line perpendicular to another at any point on it. How could you draw a line parallel to the given line and passing through the point *P*?

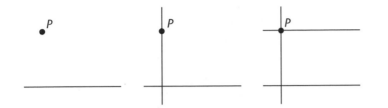

You can do it by using the set-square twice, first to create a perpendicular line through *P* and then another line through *P* perpendicular to that one. This will be parallel to the original (given) line.

You could then draw a rectangle, but you cannot draw a square, because you have no way of transferring the length of one side to an adjacent side. For that you need another tool, such as a pair of compasses.

A parallel construction	Task 95

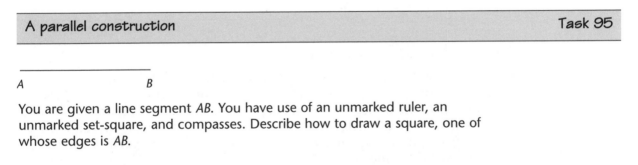

A   B

You are given a line segment *AB*. You have use of an unmarked ruler, an unmarked set-square, and compasses. Describe how to draw a square, one of whose edges is *AB*.

Comment

Use the set-square to draw a line perpendicular to *AB* at *A*. Then use the compasses with centre at *A*, radius *AB*, to draw a circle cutting the perpendicular. That gives three vertices of the square. Now use the set-square to draw a perpendicular at the new point. Use the set-square again to draw the perpendicular at *B*.

To draw a rectangle with given lengths, a similar construction would be used, but with two different sizes of circle.

In geometry, lines are imagined as carrying on indefinitely in both directions. A line segment is a portion of a line

In fact, once you have compasses, you do not actually need the set-square, because you can use the compasses to do what the set-square does.

Here is a sequence of diagrams to show how compasses are used to draw a perpendicular through the point *P*, as was done with a set-square above. Try to interpret them for yourself before reading the description given.

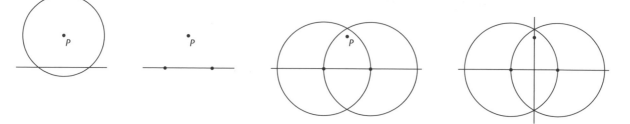

This new line is called the perpendicular bisector of the two points. It is at right angles to the line joining the points and halfway between them.

Comment

Draw a circle with its centre at *P*, and cutting the given line in two points. (That circle is now no longer needed.) Draw circles centred at the two new points, and join their two points of intersection. The result is a line perpendicular to the given line through *P*. The reason this works is that all the points on the new line, including *P*, are equi-distant from the two first-constructed points.

In mathematics this is often called invariance.

2D transformations

Many designs and patterns use transformations of shapes such as rotations and reflections, but transformations are also important because they help make clear connections between shapes and between parts of a shape. To get a feeling for reflections, rotations, enlargements and other transformations, you need to get a sense of what changes and what remains the same.

Reflecting
There are several practical methods of creating a reflection in a line. Some of them are below.

(a) Fold the page along the mirror line and prick the shape through onto the other side.

(b) Copy the shape and mirror line on tracing paper. Turn over the tracing paper and fit the mirror line on top of the original. Press through the shape on the tracing paper onto the page underneath.

(c) Take each point of the original shape and draw a corresponding point the same distance away from the mirror on the opposite side.

In the first diagram below, a polygon is shown reflected in the line. Reflect the other shape in the same line. Reflect the shapes in the second diagram. Was one pair easier to draw than the other? Why?

The significance of this is that to undo a reflection you reflect again in the same mirror line.

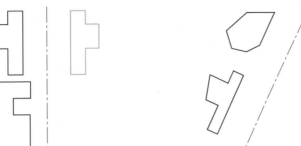

Comment

The result of a reflection is the shape you see in a mirror placed on the mirror line, viewing from the side the original shape is on. If you view in a mirror from the other side, you should, of course, see an image of the original shape.

People usually find it rather difficult to reflect a shape in a line that is not vertical or horizontal, often making the mistake of having the lines which join corresponding points horizontal rather than at right angles to the mirror line.

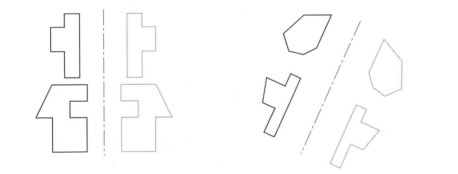

A shape is said to have a line of symmetry if that line, when used as a mirror line for a reflection, sends the shape back onto itself.

For each of the shapes shown, sketch in the mirror lines of symmetry.

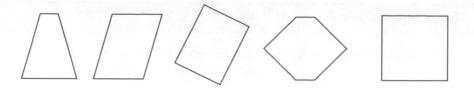

Comment

All of the mirror lines have been drawn in:

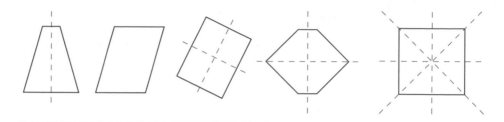

Rotating

Look again at the diagram showing tessellating triangles.

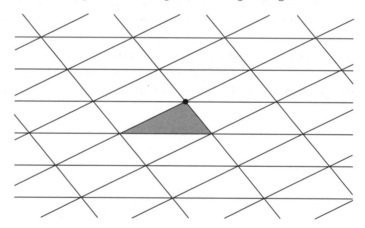

Pick the shaded triangle and any one of the others that cannot be reached by sliding the shaded triangle. These two triangles are rotations of each other. Put a piece of thin paper on top and make a copy of the original triangle on it. Find a point about which to rotate the top sheet so that the copy lies on top of the second triangle. If the triangle you chose made it easy to find the point (the centre of rotation), choose another second triangle that you think might be more difficult. Can you find the centre of rotation for any second triangle? Through what angle does the paper turn?

Every rotation is through a half turn (180°). The rotation points are always, in some sense, 'halfway' between the triangles.

Use your experience of the rotations of triangles to decide which of the following are unchanged (invariant) by a rotation:

This is useful in doing Task 100.

▶   lengths (distances between any two points);

▶   angles (between any two lines of the shape);

▶   the centre of rotation;

▶   a line through the centre of rotation.

What can you say about the distances from the centre of rotation to the top of the shaded triangle and the corresponding point on the rotated triangle?

Comment

Rotation does not change lengths, or angles. The only point which does not move is the centre of rotation. Lines through the centre of rotation will be rotated about that centre.

The distance from the centre of rotation to *any* point of the original triangle is the same as the distance to the corresponding point on the second triangle.

The centres of rotation for the tessellating triangles were quite easy to find, because all the rotations were through a half turn. When a triangle is rotated about other not-so-special angles, undoing a rotation (finding the centre of rotation) is more complicated.

Suppose triangle *ABC* has been rotated about some point to get to triangle *PQR*. How can that centre of rotation be found, and how many such centres can there be?

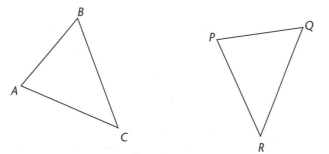

This is a useful place for you to try specialising. Rather than tackle the triangle, first start with some simpler objects.

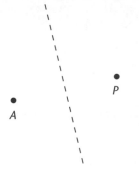

Take two points (say A and P), and try to find all points which can serve as a centre of rotation for them. Next, take two corresponding sides of the triangle (say AB and PQ), and try to find all points which can serve as a centre of rotation for them. Now use these results to help you find the centre of rotation for the triangles.

Comment

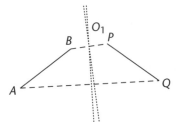

The point A can be rotated into the point P using as centre of rotation *any* point on the line perpendicular to (at right angles to) AP, and passing through the mid-point of AP (the perpendicular bisector of AP). Thus there are infinitely many choices.

To rotate A into P you must have a centre on the perpendicular bisector of AP. Similarly, to rotate B into Q you must have a centre on the perpendicular bisector of BQ. The centre of rotation must lie on each of the perpendicular bisectors, so it must be at their intersection point.

Of course, if AB and PQ are parallel, there is no such point.

But there is another rotation point because the line segment AB could be rotated so that it fits on PQ the opposite way, with A going to Q and B to P. This second rotation point will be the intersection of the perpendicular bisectors of AQ and of BP.

There are thus two points O_1 and O_2 which will act as centres for rotating the side AB of a triangle to the corresponding side PQ. The miraculous thing is, one of those points will be the centre of rotation for *any* triangle with AB as a side to rotate to a matching triangle with PQ as the corresponding side. The reason is that the rotation does not change distances and angles. So C, the third vertex of triangle ABC, which is fixed by its distances from A and from B has to follow and end up in the right place.

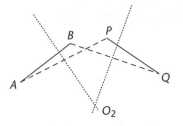

Carry out this construction on the triangles *ABC* and *PQR* above.

Translating

Look back to the tessellation of triangles on page 134. There are many copies of the original triangle which can be reached simply by sliding the triangle without turning it. These are all translations of the triangle. To specify a translation you need to specify a distance to move, and a direction in which to move. In other words, it is only necessary to specify where one point is translated to, for then every point translates by the same amount parallel to that direction.

Doing and undoing translations	Task 101

From the tessellation of triangles, pick out the original triangle and one that is translated. How could you convince somebody that it was a translation?

Comment

If you join any point to its translated point, you get a line segment Joining several points to their corresponding points will give you a collection of parallel line segments all the same length.

Scaling (enlargement)

Scaling (often called enlargement) is one of the most important transformations in geometry. It is familiar from photographs being increased or reduced in size and from scale drawings. To scale a figure all lengths are multiplied by a fixed number, the scale factor.

Scaly shapes	Task 102

Draw your own polygonal shape such as the one shown.

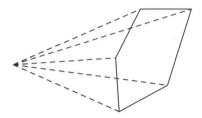

Choose some point on the page, and join it by a line segment to every vertex of your shape, as shown.

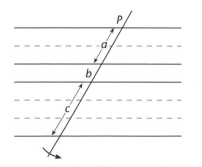

Now select a point one-third of the way along each dashed line segment from the chosen point. Join those points up in the same order as their corresponding end points to produce a new shape. What is the same about the two shapes and what is different? What is the scale factor?

Repeat for a scale factor of one and a half. What if you chose a different fraction or even a negative number?

Comment

Scaling does not change angles. It does change lengths, but all lengths are changed by the same factor. Consequently, relationships between lengths are preserved, and that is why the 'shape' stays the same. Two shapes that can be scaled into each other are called similar.

Scale factors can be whole numbers, fractions, decimals; they can be larger than one (a true enlargement: making larger) or less than one (making smaller). A scale factor of 1 would leave the shape the same size! Scale factors can also be negative: this means that you go the other side of the centre of the scaling by the corresponding amount.

A result about lengths

The ideas of scaling give rise to a result which is quite surprising.

In the diagram, the horizontal lines are equally spaced. Concentrate on the thick lines (the dashed ones are only there to show you how far apart the thick lines are). The thick lines cut the oblique line producing three line segments which have lengths a, b and c. Now imagine the oblique line being pivoted at P and swinging in the direction of the arrow. As it swings, the lengths a, b and c change. At first they all decrease until the line is vertical, and then increase again. If the rotating is stopped at any point, what are the connections between the lengths a, b and c? The perhaps surprising answer is that the lengths are always in the same multiplicative relationship:

This result is attributed to Thales (one of the six 'wise men' of ancient Greece); see Chapter 3 for more on ratio.

$a = 2b$ and $c = 3b$

Of course, this is only a special case of the result: the spacing of the thick lines can be different from those given, and there can be more than four of them. But the lengths cut off will always be in the same ratios, whatever the position of the swinging line.

This result is true because it is an instance of scaling. The diagram below shows the line from P perpendicular to the thick lines. Each of the four triangles with one vertex at P is a scaling of the others: this means that the lengths of the sides, including those on the rotating line, are also scaled versions.

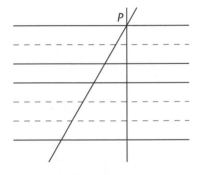

This is the basis for a method in technical drawing for dividing a line into any number of equal parts. (In the diagram the part of the rotating line between the horizontal lines is divided into six equal parts.)

Into equal parts   Task 103

Try to articulate for yourself how to divide a given line segment into a specified number of equal parts.

Comment

You should have written something like this.

Draw a line through one end of your segment and not parallel to it. Along that line, starting at the end of the given segment, draw the required number of equal segments of some length you choose. Now join the end of the given segment with the end of your last segment and call it *a*. Lines drawn through your division points and parallel to *a* will meet the given segment in the required division points.

Using coordinates

The method of locating points by coordinates enables geometrical thinking to be assisted by algebra. The standard system of coordinates in geometry requires two axes at right angles with scales the same on both axes. Points are identified by giving the distances from each axis.

Thus the pair (3, ⁻2) names the point which is found by starting at the

Coordinate grids are often called Cartesian grids and are named after Descartes (1596–1650).

See Chapter 5 for more details.

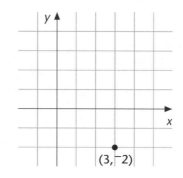

origin and travelling three units in the direction of the first axis (the horizontal axis, labelled *x*-axis), and then travelling ⁻2 units in the direction of the second axis (the *y*-axis).

Using coordinates, straight lines and circles can be represented by algebraic equations. An equation such as $y = 2x - 3$ picks out certain points (x, y). For example, it includes (2, 1) and (⁻3, ⁻9). The complete collection of points satisfying the equation gives the geometrical object (in this case a straight line). The coordinates also allow us to look at transformations algebraically.

Transforming shapes using coordinates

For more complex transformations you need advanced algebra.

For simple transformations such as reflection in the *x*-axis, the *y*-axis, or the line $y = x$, and such as rotation about the origin through 90° or through 180°, you can write down the effect of the transformations on coordinates quite easily.

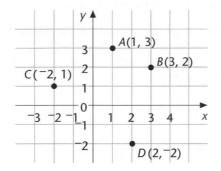

For each of the points A, B, C and D given in the diagram, work out where that point is sent by each transformation.

Transformation	A(1, 3)	B(3, 2)	C(‾2, 1)	D(2, ‾2)
Reflection in the x-axis				
Reflection in the y-axis				
Reflection in the line $y = x$				
Rotation about the origin through 180°				

Look along each row, and deduce the effect of each transformation on the coordinates of a general point.

Comment

Transformation	A(1, 3)	B(3, 2)	C(‾2, 1)	D(2, ‾2)
Reflection in the x-axis	(1, ‾3)	(3, ‾2)	(‾2, ‾1)	(2, 2)
Reflection in the y-axis	(‾1, 3)	(‾3, 2)	(2, 1)	(‾2, ‾2)
Reflection in the line $y = x$	(3, 1)	(2, 3)	(1, ‾2)	(‾2, 2)
Rotation about the origin through 180°	(‾1, ‾3)	(‾3, ‾2)	(2, ‾1)	(‾2, 2)

To reflect in the *x*-axis, you change the sign of the *x* coordinate; to reflect in the *y*-axis you change the sign of the *y* coordinate; to reflect in the line *y* = *x* you interchange the *x* and *y* coordinates; to rotate about the origin through 180° you change the signs of both coordinates.

It is not important that you remember these connections between a transformation and the changes in coordinates. What is important is that you are aware that such connections exist and that you could produce your own examples (specialise) in order to reconstruct them (or other connections for different transformations) for yourself.

Properties of 2D shapes

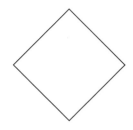

Think about the following questions.

▶ What is the name of the shape?

▶ Is a square a rectangle?

▶ What different types of quadrilateral have two lines of symmetry?

These questions indicate the kinds of confusion there can be over naming shapes. The shape here is a square, but might also be called a diamond. A square is a particular kind of rectangle, but if you were asked to draw a rectangle you would not normally draw a square. Rectangles and rhombuses have exactly two lines of symmetry, but you could say a square has two lines of symmetry (and also another two – it actually has four). Sometimes shapes are thought of as belonging to a particular class and at other times they are defined as having certain properties. Geometric reasoning involves selecting particular properties and then deducing other properties from them. For example, starting from a definition of a square as a figure with four equal sides and four equal angles, can you show that the diagonals always bisect each other at right angles?

This section concentrates on quadrilaterals – four-sided shapes – because they are the simplest shapes after triangles and so are most often put into categories and given names. The common types of quadrilateral are shown opposite:

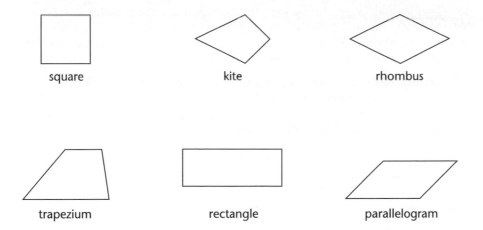

square   kite   rhombus

trapezium   rectangle   parallelogram

Recognizing shapes

The word 'quadrilateral' may make you think of a parallelogram or a rectangle or some other special type. The aim of the next task is to help you think in terms of the properties that quadrilaterals can have, and to see how these properties can be independent or can be connected.

(a)

    (i)   Draw a quadrilateral.

    (ii)   Draw a quadrilateral with one right angle.

    (iii) Draw a quadrilateral with two right angles.

    (iv) Draw a quadrilateral with three right angles.

Now go back and make sure that each example is different.

Now go back and make sure that the example at each stage is *not* an example at the previous stage.

Take care: 'two pairs of adjacent sides' does not allow three equal sides!

(b)

    (i)   Draw a quadrilateral.

    (ii)   Draw a quadrilateral with one pair of equal sides.

    (iii) Draw a quadrilateral with one pair of adjacent sides equal and one pair of opposite sides equal.

    (iv) Draw a quadrilateral with two pairs of adjacent sides equal and one pair of opposite sides equal.

Now go back and make sure that each example is different.

Now go back and make sure that the example at each stage is *not* an example at the previous stage.

Comment

In part (a) there would be no point in asking you to draw a quadrilateral with four right angles – drawing one with three right angles forces the last one to be a right angle.

Part (b) is trickier. Quadrilaterals with 'two pairs of adjacent sides' are kites. The last set of conditions forces all sides to be equal – the shape must be a rhombus and as a special case, a square.

Note the effect of the format of the task: at each stage an extra condition is imposed which draws your attention to an unnecessary assumption of simplification that many people make. Trying to draw the most general quadrilateral possible which satisfies the constraints increases your sense of the scope and nature of quadrilaterals.

A quadrilateral such as a rectangle or a parallelogram has many properties. These properties are interconnected: if a parallelogram has one right angle, then the parallel sides force the other angles to be right angles as well, and so the parallelogram must be a rectangle. The next task looks at this interconnectedness.

Task 106	Properties of a rectangle

Make a list of properties of a rectangle that you know of. Then look at the list in the comment and see which of these you have not included but which *all* rectangles do have.

Make a similar list of the properties of a parallelogram.

Comment

A rectangle has four sides – it is a quadrilateral; it has two pairs of opposite edges equal in length and parallel; it has four equal angles; it has four right angles; it has two diagonals which are equal in length; the diagonals bisect each other (i.e., intersect at their mid-points).

A parallelogram is a quadrilateral; it has two pairs of opposite edges equal in length and parallel; it has two pairs of equal (opposite) angles; it has two pairs of equal sides; it has two diagonals which bisect each other.

The interior angles of any quadrilateral add to 360°.

Once a quadrilateral has one of these properties, there may be other properties which must also be true for that quadrilateral. The initial property can force the shape to have other properties, for example:

> *A quadrilateral has four equal angles*: that forces the edges to be parallel because of properties of parallel lines, and forces the angles to be 90° since they must add up to 360°. So the quadrilateral must be a rectangle.

A parallelogram has one right angle: that forces it to have four right angles, using properties of parallel lines. So the quadrilateral must be a rectangle.

A parallelogram has equal diagonals: that forces the angles to be right angles (why?). So the quadrilateral must be a rectangle.

A quadrilateral has diagonals which are equal and bisect each other: bisecting diagonals forces it to be a parallelogram and equal diagonals forces it to have right angles. So the quadrilateral must be a rectangle.

Once again, these are not facts to remember. The important thing is to have a sense that because a shape has certain properties, others must also be true, and to be able to deduce them.

Because names and properties get mixed up, disputes can arise about how to classify shapes. Is a square a special kind of rectangle? Is a rectangle a special kind of parallelogram? It really depends whether words like rectangle and parallelogram are defined by their shapes or by their properties. The usual practice in mathematics is to define them by their properties, so any shape which has both pairs of opposite sides parallel is a parallelogram, including rectangles and squares. The next task looks at some special cases.

Special cases	Task 107

Say why the following are true.

(a) A square is a special rectangle.

(b) A rectangle is a special parallelogram.

(c) A parallelogram is a special trapezium.

Comment

(a) Rectangles have opposite sides equal and four right angles. So does a square.

(b) Parallelograms have both pairs of opposite sides parallel. So does a rectangle.

(c) Trapezia have one pair of sides parallel. So does a parallelogram.

Of course, all of the special cases have extra properties which make them special.

The word 'oblong' is often used to distinguish rectangles which are not squares.

Lengths and areas in 2D shapes

Finding lengths and areas for geometrical shapes is not about measuring them. It is about the relationships that there must be between different lengths and areas because the shapes have certain properties. These relationships are usually concerned with different lengths or areas being equal or in some particular ratio to one another. Some have already been mentioned – the connections between lengths on scaled shapes, for example. In this section various results involving lengths and areas are examined. The most famous of these relationships is probably the one known as Pythagoras' theorem.

Of course, these properties are often used in practical measuring tasks.

Pythagoras' theorem

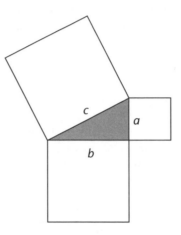

Pythagoras' theorem states that the square of the length of the hypotenuse of a right-angled triangle is equal to the sum of the squares of the lengths of the other two sides. Put another way, if you construct squares on the edges of a right-angled triangle, the area of the square on the hypotenuse is equal to the sum of the areas of the squares on the other two sides. Written algebraically, when the three sides are of lengths a, b and c as shown, it is:

$$a^2 + b^2 = c^2$$

Why is Pythagoras' theorem so important? One reason is that it enables us to calculate distances between points in the plane. Another is that it links areas, lengths and angles. It also provides the basis for being able to compare areas of polygons: break them into triangles, make squares equal in area to the triangles, then add the squares using Pythagoras' theorem to get a single square equal in area to the original polygon.

Egyptian land surveyors used a string with 12 equally spaced knots that could be held as a triangle so that there were 3 units on one side, 4 on the next and, consequently, 5 on the next. That gave them a right angle (because $3^2 + 4^2 = 5^2$) to use for marking out property.

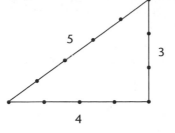

Why is Pythagoras' theorem true?

There are literally hundreds of different proofs of Pythagoras' theorem. Many of them are very algebraic, but others, like the two in the next task, use diagrams.

This task gives two visual proofs of Pythagoras' theorem. You are asked to interpret the diagrams and connect them with the theorem. Each proof works by rearranging the pieces consisting of triangles and squares.

(a)

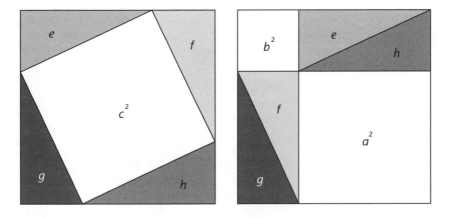

The four identical triangles in the first figure are translated to form the four in the second. Identify which sides of the triangles are a, b and c. Interpret the diagram as a statement about the area of the square on the hypotenuse as the sum of the areas of the squares on the other two sides.

(b) Where is the square on the hypotenuse? Where are the squares on the other two sides?

(c) Think about what aspects of each pair of the diagrams can change, while still remaining a proof of Pythagoras' theorum. What is particular and what is general about the diagram (what can change, and what has to stay the same in order to remain 'the same diagram')?

This proof is discussed further in Chapter 8.

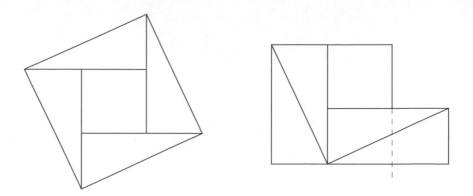

Comment

The triangles have to be right-angled, but the sides can be in any proportions. Note that these approaches to Pythagoras' theorem are algebraic in nature, even though based on diagrams.

There is a surprising variation on Pythagoras' theorem. Since what matters is the scaling rather than the shape, the theorem applies equally well to other shapes on the edges as long as they are scaled versions of each other. So it also applies, for example, to semicircles on the edges.

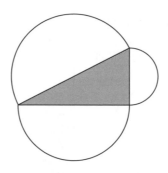

What is area anyway?

Once you start to think about it, area is a rather elusive notion. It is the amount of space contained within a boundary, which starts out as the number of copies of unit area which would be needed to make up the region.

The area of a rectangle is found by multiplying the lengths of the two sides. This works because it is a way of counting the number of unit squares which will fill a rectangle. So, a rectangle made up of four units in one direction and three in the other has an area of $4 \times 3 = 12$ unit squares.

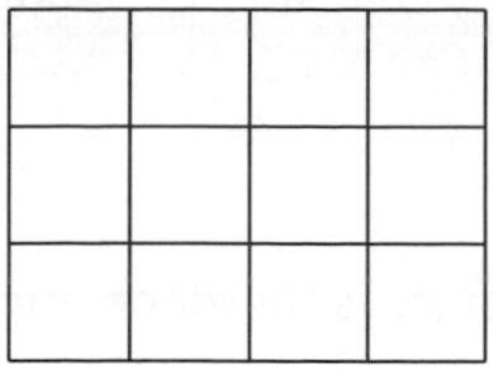

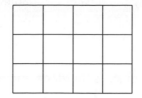

What if the sides of the rectangle were not a whole number of units? If the sides of the rectangle were fractional lengths, then the procedure would be to subdivide the unit squares into sufficiently small squares so that they would pack the rectangle perfectly. For example, a rectangle of sides 1.2 by 1.6 is shown below.

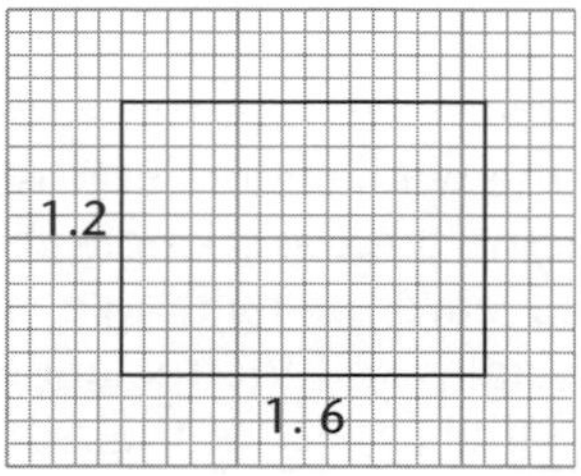

But the area formula applies even when the rectangle cannot be exactly filled by unit squares. For example, if the lengths of the sides are irrational numbers like $\sqrt{3}$ and $\sqrt{5}$ then even though you cannot pack such a rectangle with even the smallest squares, the area is the product of the two lengths. This is another example of how a definition (area) is extended from counting numbers so as to include other numbers.

Areas of parallelograms and triangles

The area of a parallelogram is $A = b \times h$, that is, the base multiplied by the height. This is a more surprising result than at first it might appear.

Area of parallelogram	Task 109

Imagine the bottom side of a parallelogram fixed, but the top side sliding along the line. The top and bottom of the parallelogram remain the same length, and the same distance apart, but the other two sides lengthen or shrink. The shape always remains a parallelogram. In one position, the parallelogram will become a rectangle (its sides will be at right angles to the base). Move the top side along again and stop. You should have images something like these.

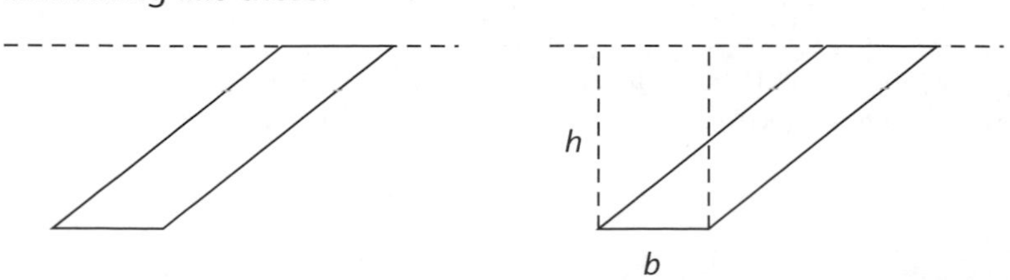

See if you can work out why the area of the parallelogram is the same as that of the rectangle, b x h.

Comment

The area of the parallelogram stays the same and is equal to the area of the rectangle (which of course is b x h). This can be seen from looking at the diagram below.

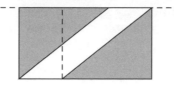

The rectangle surrounding the whole figure consists of two identical triangles and the parallelogram. Imagine the top triangle sliding to the right: it will fit above the other triangle and leave the rectangle area b x h to the left, the whole figure is now two triangles and the rectangle. So the area of the parallelogram must be the same as that of the rectangle, b x h.

The area of a triangle is:

$\frac{1}{2} \times$ base $\times$ height.

This is half of the area of a parallelogram with the same base and height. This is easy to see because any triangle is actually half of a parallelogram. It also follows that all triangles with a fixed base and height have the same area.

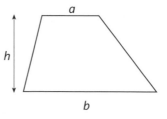

The area of a trapezium

The area of a trapezium is the distance between the parallel lines multiplied by the average (mean) of the lengths of the two parallel sides. It is:

$$\frac{h(a + b)}{2}.$$

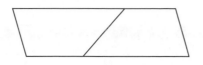

(a) You can use diagrams to show that the formula for the area of a trapezium is true. Each of the first two diagrams can be read to prove the formula. Mark in the lengths *a*, *b* and *h* on each diagram and deduce the formula:

$$\frac{h(a + b)}{2}$$

(b) A special case of the trapezium occurs when one of the parallel edges shrinks to a point. Check that this gives the formula for the area of a triangle.

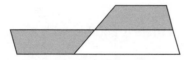

(c) Another special case of a trapezium is a parallelogram. What extra condition does this put on the lengths of the sides? Check that this can give the formula for the area of a parallelogram.

Comment

The first diagram doubles up the trapezium to make a parallelogram, whose area is $h(a + b)$. Thus the area of the trapezium is half that. The second diagram moves half of the trapezium to make a parallelogram half the height on a base of $a + b$.

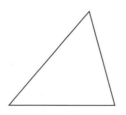

When either *a* or *b* is 0, the trapezium becomes a triangle and the formula becomes the area formula for a triangle.

A parallelogram is a trapezium with its two parallel sides equal in length. The area formula then gives:

$$\frac{h(a + b)}{2} = ha$$

which is correct for the parallelogram.

Connecting perimeter and area

Perimeter and area measure different things.

Task 111	Fixing and changing

This task involves imagining rectangles, first with a fixed perimeter and then with a fixed area.

(a) A rectangle has a fixed perimeter. Imagine it as tall and thin. Now increase the base until it is long and thin; take it back again. Think what happens to the area.

Consider each of the following statements and decide whether you think it is true (try to justify it) or false (try to find an example which shows it is incorrect).

    (i)   For any rectangle there is another with the same perimeter but larger area.

    (ii)   For any rectangle there is another with the same perimeter but smaller area.

(b) A rectangle has a fixed area. Imagine it as tall and thin. Now increase the base until it is long and thin; take it back again. Think how the perimeter changes.

Decide whether you think each of the following statements is true or false.

    (i)   For any rectangle there is another with the same area and larger perimeter.

    (ii)   For any rectangle there is another with the same area and smaller perimeter.

Comment

If you fix the perimeter, then you can make the area get smaller and smaller by making the rectangle longer and thinner. If you try to increase the area, you succeed until the rectangle is a square, and then the area will start to get smaller again as you try to adjust the sides but keep the same perimeter. So the square is a counter-example to the conjecture that the area can *always* be made larger.

If you fix the area, then the perimeter can be decreased until you get to the square, but then can get no smaller. You can make the perimeter get larger and larger by making the rectangle longer and thinner but with the same area. So again the square is a counter-example to the conjecture that you can always make the perimeter smaller for a fixed area.

Lengths and areas of circles

If you enlarge a circle of radius 1 by a scale factor of r, then the radius will become r, and the perimeter must be multiplied by r. So the ratio of the circumference to the radius must be constant, independent of the scaling. That ratio turns out to be the number 2π (or this can be taken as a definition of π). So the circumference of a circle is given by $C = 2\pi r$.

Area of a circle

Imagine the circle divided into little slices (sectors) and then re-assembled as shown in the diagram.

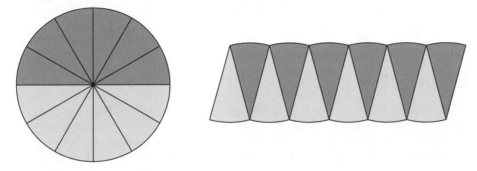

If the sectors are made thinner and thinner, the re-assembly looks more and more like a rectangle. The height of the rectangle will get close to the radius, r, and the length of the rectangle will approach

$$\frac{\text{circumference}}{2}$$

So the area of the circle will be (in the extreme limiting case):

$$\text{radius} \times \frac{\text{circumference}}{2} = r \times \frac{2\pi r}{2} = \pi r^2$$

This too can be used as a definition of π. It is a curious fact that the two numbers you get using perimeter and using area, turn out to be the same, namely, π. The number π expressed in decimals never terminates. It is known to several billion places.

For more on such irrational numbers see Chapter 2.

Parts of a circle

The sector of a circle is a slice (like a slice of a round cake).

The area of any sector is a fraction of the area of the whole circle. What fraction? It is easy to see that if the sector were a quarter of a circle, the area would be a quarter of that of the circle, and if the sector were a semicircle, the area would be half that of the circle. In fact, this idea is perfectly general. Whatever fraction the sector angle is of the whole circle, the area will be that fraction of the area of the circle.

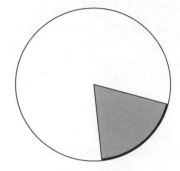

Calculations such as these are carried out (usually by a computer) to find the sizes of slices in a pie chart. See Chapter 4 for more on pie charts.

In exactly the same way, the arc length of the sector will be the same fraction of the circumference of the circle as the sector angle is of the whole circle.

Geometry in three dimensions

Although we live in a 3D world, the geometry of three dimensions is more difficult to deal with than that of two dimensions. This is partly because of the difficulty of representing solids by diagrams and descriptions, but it is also because there are more aspects to deal with in three dimensions. In two dimensions, polygons have edges and vertices. In three dimensions, polyhedra have faces, edges and vertices. In three dimensions, the equivalent of a circle is a sphere. The shortest distance joining points on a circle are straight lines, but on the surface of a sphere the shortest distances are always arcs of great circles. Again, in three dimensions there are more ways in which shapes can be symmetrical than in two dimensions.

There is no substitute for looking at and handling actual 3D shapes, and so this section can only mention some of the important aspects.

Types of 3D shapes

Even distinguishing between 3D shapes is quite tricky because there are often different ways of seeing the object. Like 2D polygons, there are different ways of classifying them – by a category or by their properties. For example, those made with flat surfaces (the polyhedra; singular, polyhedron), or those with, say, four planes of symmetry (e.g. a pyramid). One main category of solids is the prisms. These are solids which are 'the same all the way through' in cross-section, and include a cylinder, a Toblerone packet, a shoe box, and an unsharpened pencil.

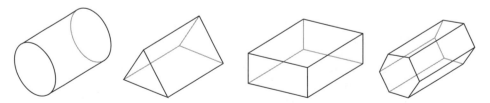

In all these solids, if a cut is made through them parallel to the end face, the result is the same shape as that face. One way of seeing a prism is to imagine the end face translated so that it sweeps out the whole solid.

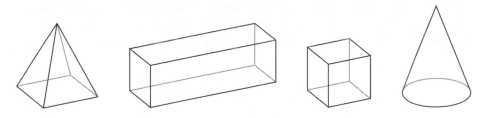

(a) Which of these shapes are prisms?

(b) See a cuboid as a prism swept out from three different 'end faces'.

(c) In how many ways can a Toblerone package be seen as a prism?

(d) In how many ways can a cylinder be seen as a prism?

Comment

The cube and cuboid are prisms, but the cone and pyramid are not. Each pair of opposite faces of a cuboid can be seen as end faces. A Toblerone package is a triangular prism in only one way: the pair of triangular ends serve as end faces. Similarly, a cylinder is a prism in only one way.

Polyhedra

The polyhedra were defined above as the group of solids which have all of their faces made of flat surfaces and their faces polygons. A cube and a pyramid are polyhedra, a cylinder and a sphere are not.

You probably will have seen examples of the incredibly varied polyhedra that can be produced.

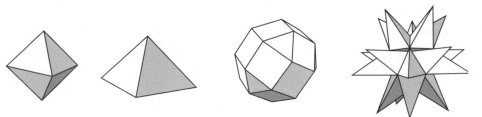

The category of polyhedra overlaps with the prisms: cubes and Toblerone packets are examples of both.

One way of constructing polyhedra is from nets which show the faces to be cut out and folded so as to form the shape. Some examples:

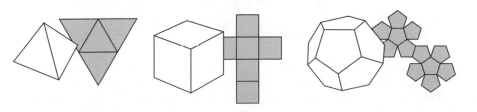

Examples of solids, including animations and nets, can be found on the Web, e.g. at http://en.wikipedia.org/wiki/Platonic_solid and http://ibiblio.org/e-notes/3Dapp/Convex.htm.

Determine what sort of shape the following nets will produce, and decide which lengths have to be equal in order for it to be a net of a polyhedron.

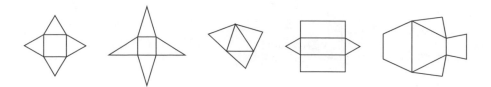

Comment

The first three are pyramids, the fourth is a Toblerone prism, the fifth is a wedge.

Properties of solids

If you do not have suitable solids to hand you could 'carve' some from a potato for example.

There is not space here to go into details of the properties of 3D shapes, but two can be mentioned: the relationship between faces, edges and vertices on polyhedra, and the symmetries of solids.

Number patterns on polyhedra

Check the following information concerning the number of faces, vertices and edges on three kinds of solids:

Solid	Faces	Vertices	Edges
Cube	6	8	12
Tetrahedron	4	4	6
Square-based pyramid	5	5	8

This surprising relationship was discovered by the German mathematician, Euler.

In each case:

faces + vertices = edges + 2

This is true for a wide range of polyhedra (but not for all of them as the following task shows).

Check whether or not the Euler relationship is true for the following:

Toblerone packet;

cylinder;

an octahedron;

a cube with a square hole cut through it.

Not all of the mirror planes are shown for each solid.

Comment

The relationship is true for the Toblerone packet and the octahedron, but not for the cylinder (not a polyhedron) or for the cube with a hole (it is not true in general for solids with holes through them).

Symmetries

As was mentioned above, there are more kinds of symmetry of a solid than of a 2D shape. Here there is only room to mention the most obvious kind: the mirror symmetry in a plane. If you imagine the solid sliced through with a mirror then the two halves must be mirror images of each other. Some examples:

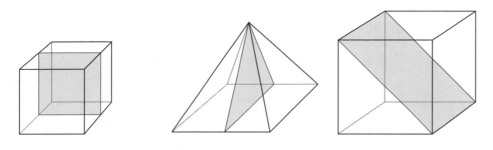

(a) Find all of the remaining mirror planes for the solids above.

(b) Find all of the mirror planes for these solids: Toblerone packet, an octahedron, a cube, a cylinder.

Comment

Answers to part (b): the Toblerone packet has 4 mirror planes, the octahedron has 9, a cube has 9 and a cylinder has infinitely many (just as a circle has infinitely many lines of symmetry). These are quite difficult to visualise, even when looking at a model of the solid. It may help to think about the positions of the mirror planes in relation to the edges and vertices of the solids.

Volumes and surface areas of solids

The volumes of cubes and cuboids are found in a manner analogous to finding the areas of squares and rectangles – by multiplying the three dimensions of height, width and depth together. Prisms are slightly more interesting because their volumes are found by multiplying the area of the base by the height. The information on other solids is best conveyed through formulas.

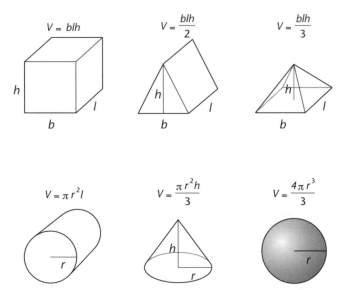

The surface area of a polyhedron is found by adding together the areas of the individual faces.

Task 116	Reflecting

Look back over the work you have done in this section. As you do so, look for instances where you think:

▶ your knowledge of geometrical relationships has increased;

▶ your ability to visualise geometrical objects has improved;

▶ your awareness of generalising in geometry has developed.

Summary

This chapter has introduced you to various aspects of geometry. It has covered:

▶ basic ideas of shape and space including some constructions and 2D transformations;

▶ properties of 2D shapes;

▶ lengths and areas of 2D shapes including Pythagoras' theorem;

▶ areas and perimeters;

▶ types of 3D shapes and their properties.

There has been an emphasis on geometric thinking through visualising and generalising.

Further study

ATM (1982) *Geometrical Images*, Association of Teachers of Mathematics.

Schumann, H. and Green, D. (1994) *Discovering Geometry with a Computer*, Chartwell-Bratt.

Johnston-Wilder, S. and Mason, J.H. (2005) *Developing Thinking in Geometry*, Paul Chapman Publishing.

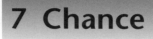

7 Chance

Introduction

This chapter looks at ways in which the notion of chance is treated in mathematics. The mathematical idea of probability enables us to describe more precisely the likelihood of chance events, especially when there are several such events happening. The sections deal with these aspects:

◗ the use of a probability scale;

◗ being clear about outcomes from events;

◗ repeated events and the idea of independence;

◗ misunderstandings in probability.

Chance and probability

It is an uncertain world where the unexpected can suddenly strike. Everyday language is peppered with words and phrases which express doubts, predict expectations or attempt to discuss the likelihood of some event. Here are some of the words and phrases in common use:

very unlikely	possible	fifty-fifty
likely	impossible	an even chance
probable	odds on	certain
quite likely		

Task 117   *Sorting chance*

Sort the above ten words or phrases in order, from least likely to most likely.

Comment

Since there can be no outcome less likely than 'impossible' or more likely than 'certain', probabilities outside the range 0 to 1 cannot occur.

For most practical purposes when chance events are being described, using words like 'likely', 'very probable' and so on provides sufficient information. However, some of these terms are quite vague and when more precise descriptions of chance events are required, a numerical scale of measure is useful. This is where chance and mathematical probability meet. Probability is a way of formalising chance where the descriptions of uncertainty are measured with numbers rather than described with words or phrases. Probabilities are measured on a scale from 0 to 1, where 0 corresponds to 'impossible' and 1 to 'certain'.

(a) Draw a probability scale like the one below. Mark on it your estimate of the numerical probabilities of the ten words and phrases used in Task 1.

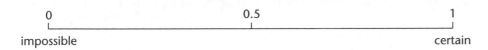

(b) imagine that a sample of people, chosen at random, were asked to do this exercise. Which words or phrases do you think would result in most and which in least agreement?

Comment

There is no single correct answer to this task but one person's solution is given below.

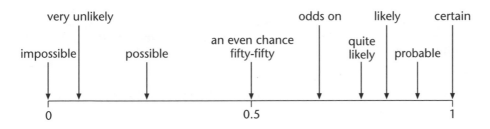

Some terms, such as 'impossible', 'certain' and 'fifty-fifty' (or 'an even chance'), are easy to position as they clearly refer to precise points on the probability scale. 'Likely' will lie somewhere between 0.5 and 1, but where to place it within this range may depend on how optimistic you are. Including 'very' in front of a probability term tends to push its position on the probability scale towards the extremes, whereas using 'quite' pushes its position towards the centre.

'Possible' is a more ambiguous word, as it depends on how you say it. Try wrinkling your nose and say with a dubious tone, 'Well, I suppose it *might* be possible', and you've suggested a low probability. Try it with an enthusiastic smile and say, 'Yes, I really think that *would* be possible', and now you're suggesting a probability between 0.5 and 1.

Outcomes

You may have wondered why textbooks on probability seem to focus on abstract situations like rolling dice, tossing coins and drawing coloured balls out of bags. When asked about the resulting outcomes, one might be forgiven for saying, 'Who cares?'. You might expect that books would concentrate on everyday events that have chance outcomes – what the weather would be like or whether the bus would be late, and so on. The main reason they do not is related to a fundamental difference between the way in which probabilities are calculated for dice and coins and for everyday events.

The probabilities of the possible events and outcomes associated with dice and coins are clearly defined and can be calculated in advance. By appealing to the symmetries of their shapes the various outcomes can be defined precisely and, corresponding to each outcome, a precise probability allocated.

'Dice' is a plural; the singular is 'die'. Although 'die' is hardly ever used in everyday speech, it is still usual in probability.

For example, a die is a cube with six faces. Since it is symmetrical, it is a reasonable assumption that each face has an equal chance of landing uppermost, and so the probabilities of rolling a 1, 2, ... , 6 are all the same.

Since it is certain that a throw must give one of 1, 2, 3, 4, 5, or 6 (i.e., a total probability of 1), each of the separate outcomes must have a probability of 1/6. This is normally written as follows:

$$P(1) = P(2) = P(3) = P(4) = P(5) = P(6) = \tfrac{1}{6}$$

Task 119	Giving a toss

Explain in your own words the following mathematical statement which describes the outcomes of tossing a coin:

$$P(\text{H}) = P(\text{T}) = \tfrac{1}{2}$$

Comment

This might be expressed as: the probability of tossing 'heads' equals the probability of tossing 'tails' and both are equal to a half.

The chance that the coin stands on its edge is so small as to be negligible.

Probabilities associated with everyday events like the weather cannot be clearly defined and calculated in this way. The best that can be done is to keep records over a period of time and count how often the various outcomes occurred. These results can then be used to predict the future. For example, the prospects for an operation might be given as 'There is a 70% chance of it being totally successful'. How is this probability arrived at? It is based on medical statistics: in all the operations of that kind given in the past, 70% have been successful. This appears to be saying that, 'If you have this operation, your probability of success is 0.7'. But there is still a further difference from probabilities with dice and coins. The actual operations carried out will not all be identical – they will have differed depending upon the condition of the patient and the ability of the surgeon, etc. Additionally, for any individual there may be other factors (unknown to the specialist) which make success more or less likely. Even the meaning of 'success' may be difficult to pin down: there may be side effects or the original condition may recur at a later time.

Dice and coins, on the other hand, are safe and dependable. This makes them a good vehicle for learning about probability and explains why they are so popular in school mathematics. Of course, any die or coin will never be completely symmetrical but it is sufficiently 'perfect' so as to represent a good model for describing and investigating situations of equal likelihood.

Outcomes are often recorded with the aid of network diagrams (sometimes called tree diagrams). For example, the simple network diagram below sets out clearly the six outcomes that could result from rolling a die. Alongside the network diagram are the associated probabilities of each outcome.

This very simple diagram helps to keep the various outcomes clear. As you will see, it is a particularly helpful way of representing outcomes when two or more dice are rolled.

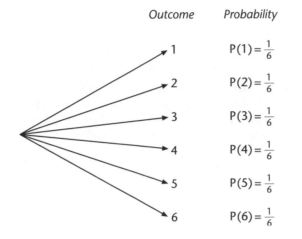

Outcome	Probability
1	$P(1) = \frac{1}{6}$
2	$P(2) = \frac{1}{6}$
3	$P(3) = \frac{1}{6}$
4	$P(4) = \frac{1}{6}$
5	$P(5) = \frac{1}{6}$
6	$P(6) = \frac{1}{6}$

More than one outcome

When outcomes are taken together the result is termed an event. More precisely, an event can be either a single outcome or two or more outcomes taken together. Here are two examples of events:

getting a score greater than 4;

getting an even score.

The probability of an event	Task 120

Based on a single roll of a die, calculate the probability of each of the following events:

(a)   the probability of getting a score greater than 4, $P(\text{score} > 4)$;

(b)   the probability of getting an even score, $P(\text{score is even})$;

(c)   the probability of getting a score greater than 6, $P(\text{score} > 6)$.

Comment

(a) You may find it helpful to think of the network diagram as branches coming out of a tree. The probability of getting a score greater than 4 is represented by the two branches corresponding to outcomes 5 and 6 and its value is the sum of the separate probabilities of these outcomes.

Expressed in symbols:

$$P(\text{score} > 4) = P(5) + P(6) = \frac{2}{6} = \frac{1}{3}$$

(b) The probability of getting an even score is:

$$P(\text{score is even}) = P(2) + P(4) + P(6) = \frac{3}{6} = \frac{1}{2}$$

(c) There are no outcomes greater than 6, so this event is impossible. That is:

$$P(\text{score} > 6) = 0$$

The idea can be taken further by considering more complicated events. For example, how would you calculate the probability of getting a score greater than 5 or less than 2? Spend a moment thinking about the use of the word 'or' here. Does it imply *more* branches or *fewer* branches on the network diagram? Does it therefore *increase* or *decrease* the likelihood?

The calculations in Task 121 invite you to put this sort of thinking to work.

Task 121	More complicated events

Based on a single roll of a die, calculate the probabilities of the following events:

(a) the probability of getting a score less than 2 *or* greater than 4, $P(\text{score} < 2 \text{ or score} > 4)$;

(b) the probability of getting an even score or an odd score, $P(\text{score is even or odd})$;

(c) the probability of getting an even score or a score less than 3, $P(\text{score is even or score} < 3)$.

Comment

The event in (b) covers all possibilities, and so is a certainty.

If you concluded that 'or' implies more branches of the tree and therefore is an invitation for you to *add* the probabilities, you were correct!

The solutions are as follows.

(a) $P(\text{score} < 2 \text{ or score} > 4) = P(\text{score} < 2) + P(\text{score} > 4) = \frac{1}{6} + \frac{2}{6} = \frac{3}{6} = \frac{1}{2}$

(b) $P(\text{score is even or odd}) = P(\text{score is even}) + P(\text{score is odd}) = \frac{1}{2} + \frac{1}{2} = 1$

(c) A common mistake here is to give the answer 5/6. This is incorrect. The problem is that the two events 'getting an even score' and 'getting a score less than 3' are overlapping; the outcome 'score = 2' occurs in each. So, simply adding the separate probabilities involves double-counting this outcome (which has a probability of $\frac{1}{6}$).

The correct answer is found by subtracting the overlapping probability, thus:

P(score is even *or* score < 3)

$= P$(score is even) $+$ P(score < 3) $-$ P(score is even *and* < 3)

$= \frac{3}{6}$ $\qquad\qquad$ $+$ $\frac{2}{6}$ $\qquad\qquad$ $-$ $\frac{1}{6}$

$= \frac{4}{6}$ $\qquad\qquad$ $= \frac{2}{3}$

Clearly this problem of overlapping events is something of a trap. The simple rule for adding events will only work for events which do not overlap. Such events are known as mutually exclusive events (i.e., the occurrence of one excludes the other). To summarise:

If two events A and B are mutually exclusive, the probability of A *or* B occurring, P(A *or* B), is equal to P(A) + P(B).

If two events A and B are *not* mutually exclusive, the probability of A *or* B occurring, P(A *or* B), is equal to P(A) + P(B) – P(A *and* B).

Repeated events

So far you have looked at outcomes and events from a single roll of a die or toss of a coin. Now, think about how you could represent the outcomes and events when a coin or die is tossed twice (two coins are tossed or two dice rolled). Although this might sound complicated, the network diagram keeps it all quite straightforward. For example, when a coin is tossed twice, the four possible outcomes (HH, HT, TH and TT) can be set out clearly as follows:

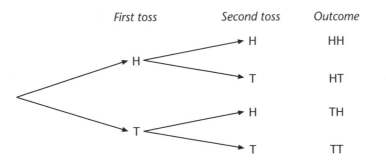

Now the network diagram has two sets of branches. It is helpful to consider them in sequence – first toss and second toss. To return to the 'tree' metaphor used earlier: just as the branches of a natural tree get smaller as they become twigs and then leaves, so too do probabilities as you move from left to right across the network diagram.

Once the outcomes have been set out clearly in this way, you can calculate the probabilities of the various events quite easily. Let us start with the first outcome of HH – i.e., heads on the first toss followed by heads on the second. What is the probability of achieving HH?

This can be understood in common-sense terms as follows.

The probability of achieving heads on the first toss is a half. This fraction further subdivides on the second toss, into a half of a half (i.e. a quarter) in each case. So,

$$P(\text{HH}) = P(\text{HT}) = \tfrac{1}{4}$$

The final column of the following diagram shows how the probabilities are calculated. For example, the probability of tossing heads twice, $P(\text{HH})$, is calculated by multiplying the two separate probabilities together, giving $\tfrac{1}{4}$.

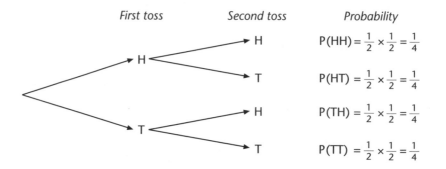

In the next task you are asked to interpret the information contained in this network diagram.

Task 122	A toss of the head

Using the network diagram above, calculate the probability of:

(a) tossing at least one head;

(b) tossing one head and one tail, in any order;

(c) tossing the same outcome on both coins.

Comment

(a) $P(\text{HH}) + P(\text{HT}) + P(\text{TH}) = \tfrac{3}{4}$

(b) $P(\text{HT}) + P(\text{TH}) = \tfrac{1}{2}$

(c) $P(\text{HH}) + P(\text{TT}) = \tfrac{1}{2}$

Independence

Probability is one area where many people's intuition lets them down. The notion of independence is a useful way of describing and debunking some common fallacies.

On a roll	Task 123

A fair coin has been tossed ten times and here are the outcomes:

H T T H T T T T T T

What would you expect the next toss to produce?

Comment

There are several possible responses to this question; here are two incorrect ones.

> Incorrect response A: 'The next outcome is more likely to be heads because there has just been a run of tails.'

> Incorrect response B; 'The next outcome is more likely to be tails because the coin seems to be on a run of tails.'

The correct answer to this question is that the coin is fair and so each toss is independent of what has gone before. Therefore the probability of tossing heads is 0.5 every time the coin is tossed. The reason that people may come up with response A could be to do with some faulty understanding of 'the law of averages'. Although it is true that, in the long run, the proportion of heads settles down to 0.5, it is certainly not the case that a short run of tails will inevitably be immediately compensated by a matching run of heads. The 'settling down' process simply does not work like that. The coin has no memory. It does not know that there has just been a run of tails. What happens is that, in a long run, any small irregularities are swamped by the nearly equal numbers of heads and tails. If the coin-tossing continued to a thousand tosses, with equally likely heads and tails, then the eight tails in the first ten tosses would be insignificant.

The mathematical term for this is independence. Repeated tossing of coins or dice are independent because the outcome of each new toss is unaffected by the outcomes of previous tosses.

The notion of independence is important when making a formal statement of the rule for multiplying probabilities. On page 165 you saw that the probability of two successive events occurring is found by multiplying the separate probabilities for each event. However, this is true only if the effect of the first event does not alter the probability of the second. In other words, the rule assumes that the two events are independent.

Bearing this in mind, the rule for multiplying probabilities can now be stated formally.

> If two events A and B are independent, the probability of A and B occurring, $P(A \text{ and } B)$, is equal to $P(A) \times P(B)$.

Common misunderstandings about probability

Here are some of the misunderstandings that many adults have.

The gambler's fallacy

As was discussed in Task 123, it is often mistakenly thought that, when a coin is tossed repeatedly, a recent run of heads is more likely to result in tails at the next toss. This is sometimes called the 'gambler's fallacy', so named because many gamblers believe it and casinos thrive on their foolishness. The fallacy can be exposed by the notion of independence. Random events like rolling dice, buying a winning scratch card or premium bond, choosing a winning set of lottery numbers, and so on, are independent of every other occasion that you do them and carry no memory from one selection to the next.

Equally likely events

A common but mistaken belief is that, if there are only two possible outcomes, they must automatically be equally likely. For example:

> 'I'm taking my driving test tomorrow. I can only either pass or fail, so I must have a fifty-fifty chance.'

Of course, this line of argument is flawed. Dice and coins yield equally likely outcomes but only because of their symmetrical shapes. If you were to toss a drawing pin repeatedly, you will discover that there are only two ways that it can land (on its side and on its back) but these are not equally likely outcomes. Try it and see!

The next task shows another instance of the same fallacy.

Task 124	Equally likely?

Suppose you wish to have a list of the results of 100 tosses of a pair of coins and to save time you use the random number key on your calculator. You ignore any digit larger than 2, and use the digits 0, 1 and 2 to represent the outcomes 0, 1 and 2 heads. What do you think the results would look like – and why would they not represent the frequencies of tossing two coins?

Comment

You should get roughly equal numbers of each outcome. But the coin-tossing outcomes are not equally likely, as you saw on page 167. The event '1 head' is actually twice as likely as the other two (because it can be formed in two ways; HT and TH).

Risk

The term 'risk' is usually used in a context where the outcomes are unwelcome. For example, you might talk about the risk of catching a particular disease but would not refer to your risk of winning the lottery. However, 'risk' is a more complex idea than merely a measure of chance. It contains a second element which takes account of the degree of severity of the consequences. For example, consider the risk involved in going out on a cloudy winter day without an umbrella. There is quite a high chance of rain and, if it does rain then you may get wet, but the consequences are not serious so you have not taken a great risk. Alternatively, you might experience a situation where the chance of the unwelcome outcome occurring is small but the consequences are serious – for example, the sort of risk that everyone runs when flying in an aeroplane. Again this is not a highly risky activity. Greatest risk occurs when both the chances of failure are high and the outcomes are serious – for example, the sort of risks attached to 'going over the top' in the First World War or agreeing to an organ transplant operation.

People are generally poor at assessing risk — this is because of a combination of factors including familiarity (or lack of it) with situations, insufficient knowledge, and media hype leading to misconceptions of likelihood. One way of assessing overall risk is to combine the effects of the likelihood of an event happening and the severity of possible consequences. One commonly used method is to rate likelihood and severity of outcome on a scale of 1 (slight) to 3 (severe) and multiply the result.

Likelihood	Severity of possible consequences		
	1	2	3
1	1	2	3
2	2	4	6
3	3	6	9

Coincidences sometimes happen

Unlikely events are more common than people tend to believe. Children, in particular, are often too quick to find alternative explanations ('That's more than just coincidence – there must be something out there!') when in fact the phenomenon may simply be one of those occasional glitches that are part of chance variation. For example, in a class of, say, 25 students there is a better than evens chance that at least two of them share the same birthday. For most people this is a surprising result. Two strangers can meet and be amazed to find that they have so many things in common (perhaps they share the same star sign, job and hobby). We should not be surprised by such coincidences. On the contrary, we should be surprised not to find them occasionally. If you toss a coin 100 times you will almost certainly get a long run of heads or tails somewhere in your results, just from chance alone. Writing some 2000 years ago, the Greek essayist Plutarch put his finger on the button when he wrote:

It is no great wonder if, in the long process of time, while Fortune takes her course hither and thither, numerous coincidences should spontaneously occur.

Task 125	Reflecting

Has your sense of probability been modified in any way by working through this section? To help you reflect, here are some phrases that you have encountered:

mutually exclusive	tree diagrams	adding probabilities
independence	successive outcomes	

You may wish to make entries on some of them in your mathematical dictionary.

Summary

This chapter has provided an introduction to the notions of chance and probability. It included:

▶ calculating outcomes from events including repeated ones;

▶ some common misunderstandings about probability, including the notion of risk.

Further study

Graham, A. (2003) *Teach Yourself Statistics*, Hodder & Stoughton.

Graham, A. (2006) *Developing Thinking in Statistics*, Sage Publications.

Haigh, J. (2003) *Taking Chances: Winning with Probability*, Oxford University Press.

Paulos, J. A. (2001), *Innumeracy: Mathematical Illiteracy and its Consequences*, Viking.

8 Proof and reasoning

Introduction

In this chapter you are asked to think about reasoning in mathematics. Mathematical reasoning is wider than just proving results; it can involve seeking answers to these questions.

▶ What is it that is true?

▶ How can I be sure? What kinds of reasons are convincing?

▶ Why is it true?

Many of the tasks in other sections of this book have involved you in one or more of these kinds of mathematical reasoning.

What is it that is true? You look for patterns or regularities and start to think a result is true. You then find more evidence for it and become convinced that it must be true; but you may not have any immediate means of justifying your conviction. In other words, you are able to make a conjecture.

How can I be sure? Just accumulating evidence is not enough: you have to be certain that there are not any counter-examples. You need an argument which will prove that the result is true. Often in mathematics, reasoning takes place in logical steps – if such and such is true, then this follows and then this, and so on. This is the activity known as proof. It is what you need to convince yourself and, perhaps more clearly stated, to convince other people.

Why is it true? If the argument is correct, a proof establishes the truth of something. But it may not help you see why something is true. A not unusual reaction to having something explained logically is, 'Well, yes, I can't fault the logic, but I don't see what makes it happen'.

For example, the lines of shaded circles in the first task of Chapter 5.

For example, the proof in Chapter 6 that angles of a triangle sum to 180°.

Recognising reasoning   **Task 126**

Look back through the tasks you have done while working on this book. Find four examples where you were engaged in mathematical reasoning.

Comment

There are many examples you might have picked out depending on which sections you did most work on. Some possibilities are:

Chapter 1, following reasoning to show that the first ten odd numbers need to be added to sum to 100 (Task 6 Undoing squaring, p. 8)

Chapter 2, the reasoning employed to extend the notion of powers and indices from positive whole numbers to negative numbers. (Index notation p. 23)

Chapter 3, the argument that, for practical purposes, the difference in the calculation method for map gradient and road gradient can be ignored (Task 50 Does it matter? p. 71).

Chapter 4, reasoning used to explain why some graphs can be misleading (Task 61 Redrawing the line graph, p. 91).

Chapter 5, reasoning involved in comparing pairs of equations to get a solution for two unknowns (p. 112).

Chapter 6, reasoning to deduce how to find a centre of rotation for two triangles (Task 100 Undoing a rotation, p. 135) .

Chapter 7, reasoning used to determine how many outcomes are possible when two coins are tossed (p. 165).

In some of the cases cited above reasoning is used to understand a situation better, in others to make sure that a general result is true in all possible cases. Mathematical proof has similar roles. Mathematicians prove results in order to establish them irrefutably as part of what is known in mathematics, but they are pleased when they prove them in ways that show how these results relate to other known results, hence organising and clarifying whole areas of mathematics.

Although proving very abstract and specialised results is hard work, proof can be used to clarify and establish quite accessible ideas. This section attempts to:

▶ help you become more aware of kinds of mathematical reasoning;

▶ make clearer several different types of mathematical reasoning;

▶ help you read proofs you may come across in mathematics texts.

What is true?

Before there can be any proof there must be something to be proved. In the next task there is no claim, just a problem. You are asked to specialise (use particular numbers) and then make a conjecture, which can be proved or disproved later in this section.

Task 127	Deciding what

Take any two numbers that sum to one.

Square the larger and add the smaller.

Square the smaller and add the larger.

Which result will be bigger?

Conjecture and then think about how you would convince someone else of the truth of your conjecture.

Comment

How many cases did you try before you formed your conjecture? Did more cases make you more sure?

Did you try fractions or decimal or positive and negative numbers or a mixture of these? Did you use algebra to express what you saw, perhaps using a and b to stand for the two numbers? What if either of a or b is zero?

Notice that 'numbers' here cannot just mean whole numbers as there would be hardly any cases, so when specialising include fractions, decimals and negative numbers in your examples.

Later in this chapter (Task 135 Return to one sum, p. 183) a proof will be given of the result which you might have conjectured.

Sometimes in mathematics, reasoning is used to decide not just *whether* something is true, but rather *when* it is true. Bear this in mind when you try the next task.

Deciding when	Task 128

Look at these three algebraic statements:

$$2x > x + 2$$
$$2x = x + 2$$
$$2x < x + 2$$

They seem to contradict each other. Does that mean they are all untrue? Or that some of them are untrue? Or might they all be true some of the time? What do you think and why? Specialise to particular values of x: try to find when each statement is true.

Comment

Perhaps the middle one is the easiest to think about. Is it possible that $2x = x + 2$?

Well, yes it is, because by treating the statement as an equation to be solved you find that $x = 2$. So a true statement is that:

$$2x = x + 2 \text{ when } x = 2.$$

Specialise? For example, when $x = 3$, then $2x = 6$ and $x + 2 = 5$.

What happens when x is more or less than 2?

In fact, if $x > 2$, adding x to both sides of the inequality gives $x + x > 2 + x$.

Therefore:

$$2x > x + 2 \text{ when } x > 2.$$

For example when $x = {}^-3$, then $2x = {}^-6$ and $x + 2 = {}^-1$.

Similarly, if $x < 2$, adding x to both sides of the inequality gives $x + x < 2 + x$.

$2x < x + 2$ when $x < 2$

The above comment has several features which are often used when something is proved in mathematics.

◗ All possible cases are considered. In this context x must be greater than 2 or equal to 2 or less than 2. There are no other possibilities.

◗ The third case starts with the word 'Similarly'. The word 'Similarly' is used to indicate that the logical structure of the argument here is the same as in the previous case.

Mathematicians like to do as little work as possible, so they look for arguments which will work in several situations. They are also fond of succinct symbols.

This example is a good illustration of how you can by logical reasoning prove something but gain little insight into why it is true. It tells you exactly which is the greater of $2x$ and $x + 2$, but offers no reason why. The proof does not make it clear, for example, whether the reason $x = 2$ is a crucial value is connected to the 2 in $2x$, or the 2 in $x + 2$, or neither, Visualising the example may give you more insight. If you draw the graphs of $y = 2x$ and $y = x + 2$ on the same axes, it shows you clearly which is the greater and when.

Drawing a graph is also useful because if you change some of the values and have, say, $x = 3$ instead of $x = 2$, it is simpler to see what the effect would be.

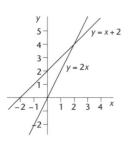

A note on notation

The most familiar, of the many symbols which are used in mathematics are probably the numerals 0, 1, 2, 3, 4, 5, 6, 7, 8 and 9 together with the decimal point '.' and the operation signs +, −, × and ÷ which make it possible to write down calculations.

You may find it helpful to include some entries on symbols and notation in your mathematical dictionary.

One very common symbol which deserves special mention is the equals sign '=' which was invented by Robert Recorde who wrote in *The Whetstone of Witte* (1557) that he had chosen this form 'because noe 2 thynges can be moare equalle'. It may seem obvious to say that it is used to show that two things are equal as in:

$2 \times 5 = 10$ or $2x = x + 2$

but it is all too often misused when a sequence of calculations is performed. For example, look at the way someone has written their workings for calculating $13 \times 5 + 24 − 7$:

$13 \times 5 = 65 + 24$

$= 89 − 7 = 82$

While you might understand what was intended, as written this is nonsense since 13×5 is not equal to either of $65 + 24$ or $89 - 7$, as is apparently claimed. What is meant is:

$$13 \times 5 = 65$$
$$65 + 24 = 89$$
$$89 - 7 = 82$$

with each intermediate answer being used as part of the next calculation.

Notice how this correctly written version contrasts with key presses when using a calculator to carry out the calculations. On a four-function calculator you would press:

13 $\boxed{\times}$ 5 $\boxed{+}$ 24 $\boxed{-}$ 7 $\boxed{=}$

As was seen in Task 128, '=' can be used when the statement is only sometimes true. Whenever you see an equation to be solved, you can read it as, 'For what values of the unknown(s) is this statement true?'.

Sometimes it is important to emphasise that a statement is always true. For this purpose the symbol '$\equiv$' is used. So, for example, you may see the statements which were written in Chapter 5 as:

$$a + b = b + a \quad \text{and} \quad a \times b = b \times a$$

written as:

$$a + b \equiv b + a \quad \text{and} \quad a \times b \equiv b \times a$$

to indicate that they are true for *all* possible values of a and b.

The first of these, $a + b \equiv b + a$, is read aloud as 'a plus b is always equal to b plus a'. Try reading the second one, one, $a \times b \equiv b \times a$, aloud.

One way of becoming confident in your use of notation is to read mathematical statements aloud.

Another symbol which looks rather like an equals sign but which has a quite different purpose is the *implication* symbol which is written '$\Rightarrow$' as in:

$$x < 2 \Rightarrow 2x < x + 2$$

The statement is read aloud as 'x is less than 2 implies that $2x$ is less than x plus 2' or as 'if x is less than 2, then $2x$ is less than x plus 2'.

The process of proving

This section examines what is needed to prove a result in mathematics, and some particular kinds of proof.

In the next two tasks the symbols $\equiv$, $\Rightarrow$ and $\therefore$ are used when appropriate.

Making reasoning more precise

In many places in this book there has been informal reasoning to show that a result is true. While these arguments are often immediately convincing, a critical person could point to assumptions that have not been proved, or cases that have been ignored. In this section two proofs are looked at more closely.

Task 129	Always true

Look at the statement below:

$$(a + b)^2 \equiv a^2 + 2ab + b^2$$

A common mistake in algebra is to write $(a + b)^2 \equiv a^2 + b^2$.

Convince yourself that it is true – perhaps by specialising, perhaps by visualising the area of a square of side length $a + b$.

Think about how you might convince someone else that it is true.

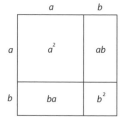

Comment

An informal 'proof' is shown in the diagram in the margin. Diagrams like this were given in Chapter 5 as a visualisation of the properties of numbers. Although they help to make clear the 'rules' of algebra, they only really make sense when a and b are positive numbers. The properties of numbers such as the commutative and distributive ones can be used to give a precise way of proving the statement for all numbers as follows.

By using the distributive property twice:

$$(a + b)^2 \equiv (a + b)(a + b) \equiv (a + b)a + (a + b)b$$

$$\equiv a^2 + ab + ba + b^2$$

This argument would be equally valid if '=' had been used rather than '≡'. However,

Because multiplication is commutative:

$$ab \equiv ba$$
$$\therefore ab + ba \equiv ab + ab \equiv 2ab$$
$$\therefore (a + b)^2 \equiv a^2 + 2ab + b^2$$

'≡' emphasises that each step is true for all values of a and b.

Sometimes results which look like algebra are really about particular lengths rather than about numbers in general. For example, Pythagoras' theorem, which is often written down in the form:

$$a^2 + b^2 = c^2$$

is about those sets of lengths which can form the sides of a right-angled triangle. Here diagrams capture much more of the generality. Look at the two diagrams opposite.

Here it would be wrong to use ≡ since it is not always true – only for certain a, b, c.

These are copies of the diagrams in Chapter 6.

Each shows four copies of a right-angled triangle together with a small square. In the first diagram the five pieces are arranged inside a square whose side is equal to the length of the hypotenuse of the triangle; in the second they are rearranged to make two squares. This claims to prove Pythagoras' theorem. A sceptical person might ask: 'How do the diagrams prove Pythagoras' theorem, and how do you know those are squares?'

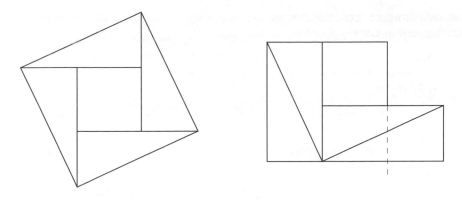

To help explain this, it is useful to assign the letters to the lengths of sides of the four identical triangles. In what follows:

c = the length of the hypotenuse (i.e., the side opposite to the right angle);

a = the length of the shortest side of the triangle;

b = the length of the remaining side of the triangle.

Proving Pythagoras   Task 130

Read the following proof of Pythagoras' theorem carefully. First, try to get a sense of the whole argument, and then look carefully at each step and work out what is being claimed.

Stage 1. What do the diagrams show?

Both diagrams are made of exactly the same pieces (four identical triangles and a small square), so they must have the same areas. The left-hand diagram is a square whose side is c. So its area is c^2. The right-hand diagram, made of the same five pieces, appears to be two squares (shown by the dashed line). One is the square on the shortest side (and so of area a^2), the other is the square on the third side (of area b^2).

Because the area of the five pieces was previously c^2 and is now $a^2 + b^2$, this proves Pythagoras' theorem, $a^2 + b^2 = c^2$. But are the parts of each diagram actually squares?

To be squares, shapes must have all sides equal and their interior angles must be right angles.

Stage 2a. Proving that the left-hand diagram is a square.

In the left-hand diagram, the sides of the 'square' are all equal because they are all the longest side of the triangle. Are the angles right angles? Each is made up of two of the angles of the triangle. Since the third angle of the triangle is a right angle and the angles of any triangle add to 180°, then those two angles must add to 90°. So it is a square.

Stage 2b. Proving that the right-hand diagram is two squares.

Both parts do have right angles at their corners (and so must be at least rectangles), but it is necessary to show that the sides are all b for the larger 'square' and *a* for the smaller. In fact, it is easy to work out the lengths using simple algebra.

On each of the diagrams, mark the lengths of the sides *a*, *b* and *c*. From the left-hand diagram, show that the length of each side of the little central square is $b - a$.

Now mark these lengths of the sides of the small square on the second diagram.

The top edge of the big 'square' is now $a + (b - a) = b$. Thus it is a square, with all sides of length *b*.

Similarly, work out the length of the top side of the small 'square'. It is the overall length, $a + b$, less the side of the large square, *b*. That is, $a + b - b - a$. So this part is also a square.

Stage 3.

The result is now proved: the parts in each diagram are squares of sides c (on the left-hand diagram) and *a* and *b* (in the right-hand diagram) and are equal in area.

Deductive proofs

Proofs that involve logical chains of reasoning, starting with what is known and going step by step to a conclusion, are known as deductive proofs. This section discusses some examples of such proofs.

Task 131	Does it follow?

In this task 'number' means 'whole number' since the phrase 'is divisible by' only applies to whole numbers.

Think about whether or not the following statements are true, then try to prove (or disprove) them.

(a) If a number is divisible by 6, then it is divisible by 3.

(b) If a number is divisible by 7, then it is divisible by 14.

Comment

(a) This is true. If a number is divisible by 6 then it can be partitioned into six equal parts. Imagine joining those six parts together in pairs; the result will be three equal parts, which is the same as saying the original number is divisible by 3.

To express this more formally, call the original number *n* and each of the six equal parts *k*. Expressed algebraically this gives:

$$n = 6 \times k = 6k$$

But $6 = 3 \times 2$ so:

$n = 3 \times 2 \times k$

In other words:

$n = 3 \times 2k = 3(2k)$

That is, n is divisible by 3.

(b) This time the statement is not true in general. To disprove it, it is only necessary to produce one case (a counter-example) where it does not work.

So, for example, the number 21 is divisible by 7 (in fact it is equal to 7×3) but it is not divisible by 14.

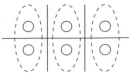

Note that even though (b) is not true in general, it is often true for particular values. For example, the number 28 is divisible by 7 and is also divisible by 14.

The true statement in (a) above could be written using the implication symbol, as:

n is divisible by $6 \Rightarrow n$ is divisible by 3.

Notice that implication does not necessarily work both ways round. In this case the converse statement:

n is divisible by $3 \Rightarrow n$ is divisible by 6

is not a true statement (using a similar argument to that in part (b) of the comment).In the next task two statements are given, together with their converses.

Arguing conversely	Task 132

Look at the two pairs of statements. Decide whether each statement in each pair is true or not. Prove each true statement using a deductive argument, and disprove each false statement by producing a counter-example.

Statement A: If m and n are both even numbers, then $m + n$ is an even number.

Converse A: If $m + n$ is an even number, then m and n are both even numbers.

Statement B: If n is an even number, then n^2 is an even number.

Converse B: If n^2 is an even number, then n is an even number.

Comment

Three of the statements are true. The exception is the converse A, for which you might have found many counter-examples, for example taking $m = 3$ and $n = 5$.

For the second pair both B and its converse are true, that is:

$$n \text{ even} \Rightarrow n^2 \text{ even} \quad \text{and} \quad n^2 \text{ even} \Rightarrow n \text{ even}$$

The two statements can be combined symbolically by writing:

$$n \text{ even} \Leftrightarrow n^2 \text{ even}$$

which is read as:

'n is even *if and only if* n-squared is even.'

You probably found converse B hardest to prove since you need to bring in some information that is not explicitly stated, namely that the square of an odd number is always odd. In a situation like this it can help to prepare for proving by organising ideas into what you know and what you want.

In this case:

I know that	n-squared is even.
I want to show that	n must be even.
I also know that (How do I know?)	the square of an odd number is odd.

So a deductive proof of converse B might go something like this.

It is shown in Chapter 1 that the nth odd number can be expressed as $2n - 1$, so the kth odd number is $2k - 1$. For example, if $k = 10$ then $2k - 1 = 19$.

Any odd number can be written in the form $2k - 1$, where k is a whole number.

So the square of an odd number is of the form $(2k - 1)^2$.

$(2k - 1)^2 = 4k^2 - 4k + 1 = 2(2k^2 - 2k + 1) - 1$ which is odd.

So if n-squared is even then n cannot be odd.

$\therefore n$ is even.

Although algebra can be a very useful way of expressing generality it does not follow that all deductive proofs are algebraic. For example, two proofs that the angle sum of a triangle is 180° were indicated in Chapter 6.

The first of these outlined a traditional proof. The next task is to make sense of a more formally presented deductive version of this proof.

This proof is in a style which many textbooks use. It sets out a deductive argument in a formal language. You will need to work through the proof line by line, but also try to get a sense of the whole. At the end you might find it useful to compare it with the version given in Chapter 6 (p. 128), and think about the different notations and methods of setting out the proof.

Theorem: The sum of the angles of a triangle is equal to 180°.

Consider the triangle *ABC* shown in the diagram.

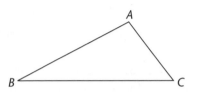

Construct a line *PQ* through *A* parallel to *BC*.

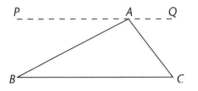

$\angle PAB = \angle ABC$ (since they are alternate angles)

$\angle QAC = \angle ACB$ (since they are alternate angles)

So $\angle ABC + \angle BAC + \angle ACB = \angle PAB + \angle BAC + \angle QAC$

But $\angle PAB + \angle BAC + \angle QAC = 180°$ (since they form a straight line)

$\therefore$ $\angle ABC + \angle BAC + \angle ACB = 180°$ as required.

Proof by exhaustion

There is another useful method of proof which is very simple to understand. It is used when there is only a small number of cases to consider, and each one can be checked. This type of proof is called proof by exhaustion. Two examples, one from probability and one from geometry, show how the method can be used.

'Proof by exhaustion' because you exhaust (use up) all of the possibilities.

Throwing two dice

Two dice, one red and one blue, are rolled and the numbers on their uppermost faces are added.

The claim here is that there are 11 possible totals and the total 7 is the most likely outcome.

Proof: The red die is represented by R and the blue die by B. The table lists all possible combinations of scores on the two dice.

R/B	1	2	3	4	5	6
1	1 + 1 = 2	1 + 2 = 3	1 + 3 = 4	1 + 4 = 5	1 + 5 = 6	1 + 6 = 7
2	2 + 1 = 3	2 + 2 = 4	2 + 3 = 5	2 + 4 = 6	2 + 5 = 7	2 + 6 = 8
3	3 + 1 = 4	3 + 2 = 5	3 + 3 = 6	3 + 4 = 7	3 + 5 = 8	3 + 6 = 9
4	4 + 1 = 5	4 + 2 = 6	4 + 3 = 7	4 + 4 = 8	4 + 5 = 9	4 + 6 = 10
5	5 + 1 = 6	5 + 2 = 7	5 + 3 = 8	5 + 4 = 9	5 + 5 = 10	5 + 6 = 11
6	6 + 1 = 7	6 + 2 = 8	6 + 3 = 9	6 + 4 = 10	6 + 5 = 11	6 + 6 = 12

By examining the results you can see that there are 11 possible totals (namely 2, 3, 4, 5, 6, 7, 8, 9, 10, 11 and 12).

Moreover, the total 7 occurs in six different outcomes which is more than any other total (in fact 2 and 12 occur once each, 3 and 11 occur twice, 4 and 10 three times, 5 and 9 four times and 6 and 8 five times each.)

Fitting squares

A domino is formed by joining two equal squares edge to edge.

A tromino is formed by joining three squares, so that each square is joined edge to edge with its neighbour.

The claim here is that there are exactly two possible trominoes.

> If two shapes are identical then one can be fitted exactly on top of the other by a combination of translating, rotating and reflecting.

Proof: Start with a domino and add one square to each of the free edges in turn as in the diagram. This generates all possible cases.

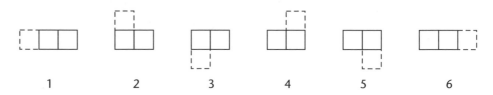

| 1 | 2 | 3 | 4 | 5 | 6 |

Cases 1 and 6 are identical.

Similarly, cases 2, 3, 4 and 5 are identical.

There are therefore exactly two distinct trominoes.

Task 134	Exhausting possibilities

A tetromino is formed by joining four squares, so that each square is joined edge to edge with its neighbour.

Prove that there are exactly five tetronimoes.

Proving conjectures

Finally, a return to Task 127 Deciding what (p. 172) from this section which was left unfinished, and a task to challenge your understanding of reasoning and proof.

Look at your notes for Task 127. See if you can use any of the ideas you have met in this section to clarify the thoughts you had then.

Next, read through the comment below and then the text that follows it. You should try to get a sense of the whole proof and also see what each step contributes.

Comment

When you attempted the problem you should have found that for each pair of numbers a and b that you chose then:

$$a^2 + b = a + b^2$$

and the more numbers you tried, the more convinced you were likely to be. However it is clearly impossible to attempt a proof by exhaustion. A deductive proof is shown below.

The formal proof is set out with informal thinking and comments side-by-side.

Informal thinking	Theorem
I want to show that $a^2 + b = a + b^2$	$a + b = 1 \Rightarrow a^2 + b = a + b^2$
The plan: I can't assume that $a^2 + b = a + b^2$, so I will take each side of it separately and show they are the same. I know that $a + b = 1$, so I can write $b = 1 - a$.	Proof $a + b = 1 \Rightarrow b = 1 - a$
By substituting for b, I can express both sides of the equation in terms of a. I put $b = 1 - a$ into the left-hand side and simplify it using algebra.	So for any pair of numbers a and b which sum to 1: $\begin{aligned} a^2 + b &= a^2 + (1 - a) \\ &= a^2 - a + 1 \end{aligned}$
I put $b = 1 - a$ into the right-hand side and simplify it using algebra.	$\begin{aligned} a + b^2 &= a + (1 - a)^2 \\ &= a + 1 - 2a + a^2 \\ &= a^2 - a + 1 \end{aligned}$
Both sides are the same, $a^2 - a + 1$.	It follows that: $a^2 + b = a + b^2$ and hence the conjecture is proved.

Here is one more result to be proved.

Task 136	Sum challenge

The sum of the first n numbers is equal to half of the sum of n^2 and n.

Remember to try and 'get a sense of' what this statement is saying – perhaps by specialising in some way. Try to express the statement algebraically and think about what you know and what you want.

Comment

Read through the discussion below. Again, try to follow the argument as a whole and also work out why each step is there. Does the train of thought correspond to your own or did you take another route? Perhaps you noted other aspects from those mentioned.

First, the claim is written more succinctly using algebra. The nth counting number is n so the statement is now written as:

$1 + 2 + 3 + \ldots + (n - 1) + n = \frac{1}{2}(n^2 - n)$

Note: $\frac{1}{2}(n^2 + n)$ can be rewritten as $\frac{1}{2}n(n - 1)$

$1 + 2 + 3 + \ldots + (n - 1)$ can be visualised as a growing triangle:

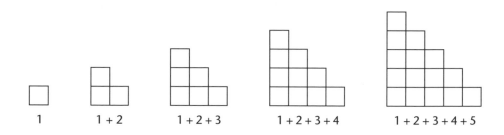

| 1 | 1 + 2 | 1 + 2 + 3 | 1 + 2 + 3 + 4 | 1 + 2 + 3 + 4 + 5 |

The numbers formed are in fact known as the triangular numbers.

Try comparing the result with the formula for the area of a triangle. (See Chapter 6, p. 149.)

and if two copies of, say, the 5th triangle are put together a 6 × 5 rectangle is obtained:

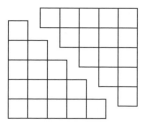

Which show that the fifth sum is equal to half of 6 × 5.

It is possible to 'see' that the same process can be used for any of the triangle numbers – but not to draw the nth case. Once more algebra can be called upon to deal with the general case.

Symbolically this is written as $\sum\limits_{1}^{n} n$ – read as 'the sum of n numbers from 1 to n'.

Let s = the sum of the first n counting numbers.

Then:

$$s = 1 + 2 + 3 + \ldots + (n - 2) + (n - 1) + n$$

Reversing this gives:

$$s = n + (n - 1) + (n - 2) + \ldots + 3 + 2 + 1$$

Adding the two versions together reveals n pairs of numbers with each pair adding to $(n + 1)$.

So:

$$2s = n(n + 1)$$

Alternatively, you may have 'seen' the pairs, of them, as shown below:

$$s = 1 + 2 + 3 + \ldots + (n - 2) + (n - 1) + n$$

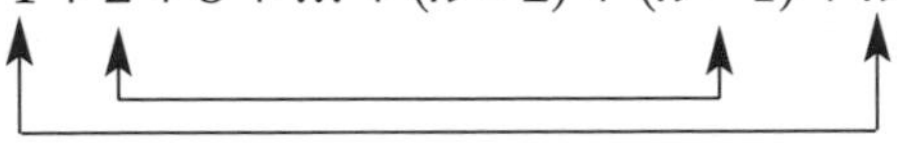

From which:

$$s = \tfrac{1}{2} n \times (n + 1)$$
$$= \tfrac{1}{2} (n^2 + n)$$

as required.

Reflect and connect   Task 137

Look back over your work on 'Proof and reasoning'. Make brief notes on any new things you have learned or new connections you have made, updating your Mathematical dictionary as necessary.

Summary

This chapter covered the nature of logical reasoning, conjectures, and formal mathematical proofs including deductive proofs and proof by exhaustion.

Further study

Burton, L. (1994) *Thinking Things Through*, Blackwell.

Mason, J., Burton L. and Stacey, K. (1996) *Thinking Mathematically*, Addison-Wesley.

9 What next?

Introduction

This chapter suggests some simple study techniques for those facing an examination, and some possible avenues for pursuing your mathematical thinking further. This book is designed to be a self-study text with stand-alone chapters that can be used in a variety of ways. How you are using the book will depend on your particular needs. This chapter explores some possible uses, some strategies that you may find useful in the future, and some suggestions for what you might do next.

As with all the chapters in this book, have a scan through the various sections and decide which ones most closely match your current needs:

▶ revision – revising particular topics, perhaps in order to pass a basic mathematics test

▶ confidence building – gaining confidence in a range of topics, perhaps in preparation for working with young learners;

▶ preparation for further study – extending knowledge and understanding of basic mathematics in preparation for further study of mathematics or mathematics education.

Strategies

Depending on how you have used the book, you will have come across some or all of the following strategies for understanding mathematics and using it to solve problems:

▶ what is the same and what is different;

▶ stressing and ignoring different aspects of a problem;

▶ sense making – using mental imagery, making connections using different presentations (saying, drawing, symbols ...);

▶ doing and undoing;

▶ what you know – what you want;

▶ specialising and generalising.

Revision

When you selected the topics to study in this book you probably used a mixture of the contents page and the index. Some of the topics may have been new to you while others were vaguely familiar. Revision is not the same as learning something for the first time. When you are working on a new topic you need to make notes because these will be used when you need to revise. Remember, revision techniques are designed to support revisiting a topic and not to learn it from scratch.

There are a number of ways that you can revise mathematics but it is vital that you plan your revision to make sure that you have enough time.

▶ Write a revision timetable. Your plan will not be the same as anyone else's because you have to take into account your personal and time commitments.

▶ Revision should be active and you will need to work through relevant activities, examples and problems.

▶ Make spray diagrams to show the connections between various topics. Condense the notes you made during the course into briefer ones.

▶ Answer questions from a past and specimen paper. Complete one of the past or specimen papers under examination conditions.

▶ Summarise the important ideas or techniques.

▶ Make a collection of cards each containing a technical term or the name of a technique. When you have a moment, choose a card and try to tell yourself what it means, where it is used, and construct a typical problem or task that makes use of it. You can also take two cards and try to construct a sequence of sentences which make mathematically coherent sense so that the first word is in the first sentence, and the last word is in the last sentence. You can also take three cards and then look for features which distinguish one of the words from the other two.

You will probably find that revision is more effective if you vary the activity and take frequent breaks, for example, general reading, making a spray diagram to summarise your notes on a particular topic, practising questions from specimen papers.

Practice with a purpose

Practising examination questions serves a number of purposes. It highlights the types of questions you need to look at in more detail. It also gives you the opportunity to develop fluency and speed. An examination has only a limited amount of time and you will need to be fluent in some mathematical techniques in order that you do not waste time.

Mathematics questions usually include words that are used differently from the way they are understood in everyday life. Look out for these words because they will give you a clue about what you need to do. For example, 'write down' or 'state' mean that you do not need to show detailed working out whereas 'find', 'calculate' or 'evaluate' require you show your working using appropriate mathematical methods and techniques.

You can also make up questions of a similar type to give you more practice. Try and make up an example of a question that is easy and another that is hard; construct 'typical' questions of each type, and articulate to yourself what it is that makes a question 'of that type'.

There are a large number of published books containing practice questions that are designed to help you improve your speed and fluency. You could couple this with the revision card strategy mentioned earlier. You can take a set of exercises and construct the most general or most typical examples of them. If you put these on cards, then you can pick a card and try to recall what technique(s) the exercises of that type used to find the answer.

Confidence

Many people believe that the key to success in mathematics is being confident. But how do you become confident when working on mathematics? It does not mean doing questions that you find easy! It means placing your trust in your mathematical thinking rather than in knowing how to do all the questions that could come up. You need to tackle questions that will challenge you and move your thinking forward.

One of the things that saps people's confidence is being stuck, and not knowing what to do when that happens. Everyone gets stuck when they do mathematics. You need to be able to recognise that you are stuck and to have some strategies come to mind for getting unstuck. Being stuck often results in feelings of anxiety or panic. People have reported a pounding heart, sweating palms or feeling like your brain has frozen. There are ways to keeping yourself calm. There is advice on 'being stuck' in Chapter 1; but here are some suggestions for use in a test situation.

- Check you understand the question. Highlight significant words. Write down what you know and what you are trying to find out.

- Break the problem into smaller steps and deal with each step in turn.

- Draw a diagram.

- Do a different question – you can go back to the tricky one if you have time at the end.

Make sure that you practise doing questions until you feel you have mastered a particular technique. It is not possible to say how many questions you will need to do. When you can tell yourself what a typical question of that type is like, and how to recognise it, you are well on the way. You are aiming for fluency and for examinations speed as well.

If you are not sure what you need to study or revise then use the self-assessment questions in the final chapter.

Preparation

Any further study that you may consider will depend on your personal circumstances and the way you prefer to learn. Some people feel they need face-to-face teaching while others find that a supported distance education course is more suitable. Courses at many colleges and most universities have prerequisite qualifications. The Open University undergraduate courses do not have prerequisite qualifications but it is advisable to study Level 1 courses prior to Level 2.

Further Education

Your local further education (FE) college will offer a variety of courses. These include basic numeracy skills, GCSE and A level mathematics. To find out more about FE courses in your area contact your local FE college or Learndirect online at

http://www.learndirect.co.uk/.

The Open University

The Open University (OU) offers a wide range of courses in mathematics and mathematics education. Unlike face-to-face universities, students at the OU sign up for individual courses rather than a whole certificate, diploma or degree. Some of the courses are listed below but you will need to check the website for up-to-date information.

Although the OU is a distance education university, many of the courses include face-to-face tutorials. The OU also provides support in the form of a personal tutor who students can contact by telephone and email.

Mathematics

Y162 *Starting with Maths* is a course designed to help you feel more confident in using mathematics in a variety of different situations – at home, in work or in your other studies. There are three main themes developed in the course:

▶ improving your mathematical skills including using a calculator effectively;

▶ developing problem-solving strategies so that you know what to do when you get stuck;

▶ practising general study skills to help you become an effective learner.

MU120 *Open Mathematics* is a course that will help you to integrate mathematical ideas into your everyday thinking, and to build up your confidence in both using and learning mathematics and in studying at a distance. It is about the relationship between mathematics and the world in general and assumes only the literacy and numeracy skills needed in everyday life. You are *not* expected to have any skills in algebra before the course starts. The skills it introduces will be valuable to those who intend to specialise in mathematics courses, even if they have met some of the mathematical concepts and techniques before. It is also suitable for all those who will be users of mathematics in other areas, such as computing, science, technology, social science, humanities or education.

Mathematics education

The OU has a number of mathematics education courses (ME code), which are all at higher education Level 3. When studying these courses you will:

- increase your mathematics subject knowledge;
- get experience of different teaching approaches and the learning opportunities they afford; and
- develop your awareness of, and facility with, ICT in the learning and teaching of mathematics.

MEXR624 *Developing mathematical thinking at Key Stage 3*. This is a one-week residential school course which is designed for anyone working with Key Stage 3 pupils.

ME624 *Teaching mathematical thinking at Key Stage 3*. This supported distance-learning course is designed for anyone working with Key Stage 3 learners of mathematics.

ME625 *Developing algebraic thinking*. This course is designed to help you develop your knowledge, appreciation and understanding of the teaching of algebra at Key Stages 2 to 4. It will broaden your ideas about how people learn and use algebra.

ME626 *Developing statistical thinking*. This course will help you develop your knowledge, appreciation and understanding of the teaching of statistics at Key Stages 2 to 4. It will broaden your ideas about the 'big ideas' of statistics and how people learn and use them.

ME627 *Developing geometric thinking*. This course is for anyone who is interested in developing their knowledge and understanding of the teaching of geometry at Key Stages 2–4. It will broaden your ideas about how people learn and use geometry

If you study enough of these Mathematics Education courses you could be awarded an Open University *Graduate Diploma in Mathematics Education*. If you combine the Mathematics Education courses with OU Mathematics Courses you could be awarded the honours degree of Mathematics and its Learning. See the OU website for more information.

The OU also has a course that is designed for people working in early years childcare and education.

E230 *Ways of knowing: language, mathematics and science in the early years*. This course is for people working in childcare and education, including: early years teachers (especially if you do not have qualified teacher status); teaching assistants; nursery nurses; playgroup workers and leaders; childminders; and others working voluntarily in school, early childhood and out-of-school settings. By the end of the course you will have:

- developed your subject knowledge in the three essential curriculum areas of language, literacy and communication, mathematics and science;

- developed your understanding of issues, theories and research which underpin practice in supporting children's learning in the three subjects;

- developed and demonstrated the sound knowledge and critical understanding of relevant theory that underpins good practice in supporting children's learning.

Books and web sources

Sources that have been mentioned at the end of relevant chapters are included in the following list of suggestions for further study.

Books

Burton, L. (1994) *Thinking Things Through*, Blackwell.

Cooke, H. (2003) *Success with Mathematics*, Routledge. *Success with Mathematics* provides preparation for bridging the gap between school and university level mathematics.

Developing Thinking in … a series covering the 'big ideas' and pedagogy of algebra, geometry and statistics, including using ICT for teaching and learning.

Graham, A. (2003) *Teach Yourself Statistics*, Hodder & Stoughton. *Teach Yourself Statistics* covers basic statistics including uses in everyday life.

Graham, A. (2006) *Developing Thinking in Statistics*, Sage Publications.

Graham, A.T. (2003) *Basic Mathematics*, Teach Yourself. *Basic Mathematics* is aimed at teaching you the mathematics you need to know for everyday living.

Graham, L. and Sargent D. (1981) *Countdown to Mathematics*, volume 1, Prentice Hall. *Countdown to Mathematics* volume 1 includes a module on basic skills and techniques in arithmetic and algebra. It includes diagnostic questions, plenty of examples to try yourself, and full solutions.

Graham, L. and Sargent, D. (1981) *Countdown to Mathematics*, volume 2, Prentice Hall. *Countdown to Mathematics*, volume 2 continues the development of skills and techniques of algebra and introduces the basic ideas of geometry and trigonometry.

Haylock, D. (2006) *Mathematics Explained for Primary Teachers*, Sage Publications. *Mathematics Explained* is written for primary teachers to enable them to deepen their knowledge and understanding and includes key teaching points.

Johnston-Wilder, S. and Mason, J.H. (2005) *Developing Thinking in Geometry*, Paul Chapman Publishing.

Mason, J. (1999) *Learning and Doing Mathematics*, Tarquin Publications. *Learning and Doing Mathematics* provides access to typical modes of mathematical thinking together with advice on how to make use of them when studying.

Mason, J., Burton, L. and Stacey, K. (1985) *Thinking Mathematically*, Prentice Hall. *Thinking Mathematically* offers experiences of mathematical thinking processes which elaborate the ideas in Chapter 1.

Mason, J.H., with Graham, A. and Johnston-Wilder, S. (2005) *Developing Thinking in Algebra*, Paul Chapman Publishing.

Websites

http://mcs.open.ac.uk/SkillMath/
The Open University Skillmath website provides a portal to a variety of mathematics, mathematics education, resource and study skill sites.

www.nrich.maths.org/
NRICH is a website with a wide range of investigative mathematical problems to work on and discuss with other users.

References

Gattegno, C. (1977) *What We Owe Children*, Routledge and Kegan Paul.

Stevens, S. (1946) 'On the theory of scales of measurement', *Science*, vol. 161, pp. 677–80

Tahta, D. (ed.) (1972) *A Boolean Anthology Selected Writings of Marl, Boole on Mathematical Education*, ATM.

A supplementary self-evaluation guide to assessing your mathematical subject knowledge and understanding

Introduction

Welcome to the 'Guide to assessing your mathematical subject knowledge and understanding' chapter, which is designed to help you get started on some mathematical work before the formal start of any course you may be taking. If you have not studied for a while, this will help you to get organised and will also help to reduce the amount of work to be done during the course.

Requirements

Your course may have specific mathematics requirements. For example, if you are training to be a teacher, you will need to take the QTA Numeracy skills test. (See http://www.tda.gov.uk/Home/skillstests.aspx for more details.)

Mathematics GSCE grade C (or equivalent) is one of the qualifications required for acceptance on a training course leading to qualified teacher status (QTS). You may well feel therefore that the knowledge you have is sufficient to enable you to teach mathematics at primary level or to support learners at secondary level. However, in order to teach or support effectively your knowledge and understanding needs to be sufficiently complete and relevant to meet the needs of the children you will be teaching, particularly in the following areas:

▶ number and algebra;

▶ mathematical proof and reasoning;

▶ measures;

▶ shape and space;

▶ probability and statistics.

You are advised to start work on self-auditing your mathematical knowledge and understanding and working towards the required mathematical knowledge as soon as is practical.

Needs assessment

This guide is designed to help you audit your current competence and suggest ways that you can overcome any deficiency by using this book. If you are particularly concerned about aspects of your mathematics then you may also need a higher-level GSCE textbook or study guide to provide additional practice examples.

If you have particular difficulties, additional help may be available from your course provider either face to face or via electronic conferencing.

Using this guide

The remainder of this guide is in two sections.

1 'Reviewing your current mathematical knowledge and understanding', which aims to help you identify any area(s) of weakness.

2 A 'Practice assessment test', which has an example of the type of questions you will need to be able to answer when your mathematics knowledge and understanding is formally assessed by your course provider.

In 'Reviewing your current mathematical knowledge and understanding' there is a series of activities for you to audit your current knowledge and understanding, which is also cross-referenced to previous sections of the book. You may find that there are topics of which you have little or no knowledge. This may be because you achieved your mathematics qualification some time ago, or the topic was not covered in the particular syllabus you followed.

For each activity you will be asked to assess your own competence and confidence. It is possible to get correct solutions without fully understanding! Only *you* can assess whether you are confident in applying your knowledge and skills. (A good strategy is, after you have tried all the questions, to go back through them and see if you think you could answer a different question 'like' that; then try to construct a testing question of the same sort or type. If you are in contact with a colleague, try exchanging questions.)

The 'Practice assessment test' is for you to use once you are confident in your mathematical knowledge and understanding. It is worth doing this under 'test conditions' to prepare yourself for any formal assessment which may be timed.

Reviewing your current mathematical knowledge and understanding

Using the audit questions to plan future work

You should work through all the audit questions, doing what you can (but without looking at the answers).

Check your answers, and as you do, note down what you feel about each topic, perhaps deciding a priority 1–5 using the following scale.

1   New to you – need to learn from scratch.

2   Something with which you recall having difficulties in the past.

3   A bit rusty – need some practice.

4   Not a problem to do, but need to check on understanding.

5   Thoroughly familiar and fully understood.

You could do this in the margin on your working page. Once you have completed and marked the audit you can make a prioritised list of topics – doing this will enable you to make best use of the revision time you have available.

The solutions are cross-referenced to pages in the previous chapters to enable you to look up particular topics. However, if you find that you have a number of deficiencies within a mathematical topic it may be better to work through a whole section.

Once you are fully confident that your skills, knowledge and understanding are to the level required, then try the practice test.

Audit

Work through the following audit questions doing what you can without looking at the answers. Do not worry at this stage if something is unfamiliar, you cannot remember something you once knew, or you are just unsure: just go on to the next question. The purpose is to identify what you need to learn or revise in the next few weeks.

The real number system

1 Put the following numbers in numerical order as they would appear on a number line:

$\frac{1}{3}$, 3^2, $-\frac{1}{3}$, $^-0.3$, 3^{-2}

2 Say whether each of the following four statements is true or false: correct the false ones as necessary.

(a) $0.2 \times {}^-0.3 = 0.6$

(b) $\frac{4}{15} - \frac{7}{20} = -\frac{25}{300}$

(c) $1\frac{3}{4} \div 4\frac{2}{3} = \frac{21}{56}$

(d) $65 < 21$

3 Draw an outline number line which indicates all numbers between 17 and 35 (including 17 but not including 35).

4 Write the following in index notation:

   (a) 10 000

   (b) 0.001

5 (a) Write 256.87 in standard form (scientific notation).

   (b) Write 0.0045 in standard form.

   (c) Write the product of your previous two answers in standard form.

6 Take the number 31.567 and write to:

   (a) the nearest whole number;

   (b) two decimal places;

   (c) one significant figure.

7 Write $\frac{1}{9}$ as a recurring decimal.

8 What type of number is $\frac{1}{4}$ when converted to a decimal?

9 Why is (i.e., 0.3333.) a rational number?

10 Why is $\sqrt{2}$ an irrational number?

11 What type of number is π?

Number operations and algebra

12 On different calculators, the following key presses can produce different answers: 2 $\boxed{+}$ 3 $\boxed{\times}$ 4 $\boxed{=}$

   A simple calculator gives the answer 20, but a scientific one gives 14. Explain how these answers occur.

13 Calculate each of the following, without using a calculator:

   (a) $32 + 2 \times 5 + 6 =$

   (b) $(32 + 2) \times 5 + 6 =$

   (c) $(32 + 2) \times 5^2 + 6 =$

   (d) $(20 + 7)(10 + 5) =$

   (e) $\frac{27 \times 1.08 \times 6.4}{1.2 \times 7.2 \times 2.4}$

14 Three people who share a house decide to split a £70 food bill between them, taking into account the number of meals eaten at home. They agree that it should be split in the ratio 2 to 3 to 5. How much does each person pay?

15 An article costing £300 is in a sale at £225. By what percentage has it been decreased?

16 What are the prime factors of 396?

17 Factorise the expression $5a^3b^2 + 5ab^3$.

18 Use the formula $C = \frac{5}{9}(F - 32)$ to calculate the Fahrenheit temperature equivalent to 15 °C.

19 Which of the following expressions are equivalent?

(a) $(3a - 3)(a - 1)$

(b) $3a(a - 2) + 3$

(c) $3a^2 - 6a + 3$

(d) $3(a - 1)^2$

(e) $3[a(a - 2) + 1]$

20 For the sequence of odd numbers 1, 3, 5, 7 ...

(a) What are the next 3 numbers?

(b) What is the nth term?

(c) What is the sum of the first n terms?

Equations, functions and graphs

21 Calculate the number(s) that satisfy the following conditions:

(a) Two more than a number is the square root of 9.

(b) The sum of a number and its square is 12 more than its double.

(c) The sum of two numbers is 5 and their product 6.

(d) $3y = 2x + 7$ and $y = {}^-2x + 1$

22 On a square grid, plot the points $({}^-2, {}^-1)$ and $(1, 2)$ and draw a straight line passing through both points.

(a) What is the y-intercept of the line?

(b) What is the gradient of the line?

(c) What is the equation of the line?

23 On the same grid as question 22, plot the graph of the function $y = {}^-3x - 1$.

(a) What is the y-intercept of this line?

(b) What is the gradient of the line?

(c) What are the coordinates of the point where the two lines intersect?

Mathematical reasoning and proof

24 What do the following symbols mean?

(a) $=$

(b) $\Rightarrow$

(c) $\equiv$

(d) ∴

(e) ≈

(f) ≥

25 Prove or disprove the following using deductive proof, proof by exhaustion or counter-example as appropriate:

(a) Numbers divisible by 9 are also divisible by 3.

(b) Any quadrilateral with a pair of parallel sides is a parallelogram.

(c) There are 11 possible totals from adding the numbers on two six-sided dice.

Measures

26 What are the Système Internationale (SI) prefix and symbol for 10^6?

27 1 UK gallon ≈ 4.55 litres.

(a) If fuel costs 75p/litre, how much is this in £/gallon?

(b) Convert 20 litres to gallons.

28 If a temperature is given as 50° ± 5°, what is the relative error for this reading?

29 A cube has a side of 2 cm.

(a) What is the area of one face?

(b) What is the volume?

30 On a map with a scale of 1:25 000 the distance between two places is 50 mm. What is the actual distance on the ground in kilometres?

Shape and space

31 What is a reflex angle?

32 Calculate all the angles in the following diagram:

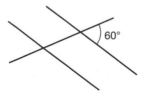

33 For each of the following shapes draw in all the line(s) of reflective symmetry:

(a)

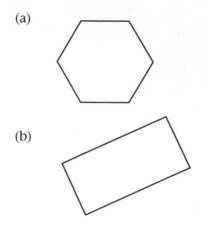

(b)

34 Which of these shapes are similar and which congruent?

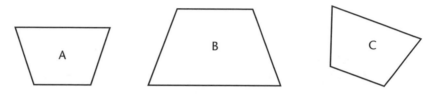

35 How many times must a square be rotated through 90° in one direction to return to its original position?

36 What is the length of the hypotenuse of a right-angled triangle where the other two sides are 5 cm and 12 cm?

37 Give three properties of a rectangle involving

(a) the sides

(b) the angles

(c) the diagonals.

38 What is the formula for the area of this trapezium?

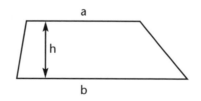

39 What is the area of a 3, 4, 5 right-angled triangle?

40 Draw the net of a 3, 4, 5 right-angled triangular prism that is 2 units long.

(a) What is the volume of the above prism?

(b) What is the total surface area of the prism?

41 The diagram shows a circle of radius 3 cm. The shaded sector is one third of the circle.

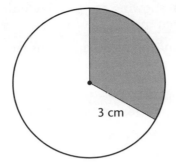

3 cm

(a) What is the area of the sector?

(b) What is the length of the perimeter of the sector?

42 A regular octahedron has eight faces and six vertices; how many edges does it have?

43 What shape are the faces of a regular dodecahedron?

Probability and statistics

44 Explain the difference between a bar chart and a histogram.

45 What does the area of a pie chart represent?

46 Name the key features of the following box plot (box and whisker diagram).

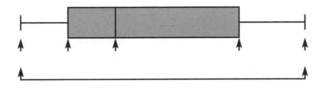

47 Using the data tabulated below calculate:

(a) the median;

(b) the mode;

(c) the mean.

Height h	Number
$120 \leq h < 130$	9
$130 \leq h < 140$	42
$140 \leq h < 150$	69
$150 \leq h < 160$	34
$160 \leq h < 170$	6

48 Draw a tree diagram showing the possible outcomes of throwing a six-sided die and then tossing a coin.

49 Explain the terms 'independent' and 'mutually exclusive' events.

Using solutions

As you check your solutions remember to decide a priority 1–5.

1   New to you – need to learn from scratch.

2   Something with which you recall having difficulties in the past.

3   A bit rusty – need some practice.

4   Not a problem to do, but need to check on understanding.

5   Thoroughly familiar and fully understood.

You could do this in the margin on your working page.

Alongside each solution is a reference to the pages in the previous chapters where you can find help on that topic, for example [page 43]. Use these to plan your revision after you have marked the whole audit and assessed your needs.

Audit solutions

The real number system

1

⁻0.33...,	⁻0.3	0.11 ...	0.33 ...	9
$-\frac{1}{3}$	⁻0.3	3^{-2}	$\frac{1}{3}$	3^2
		$\left(\frac{1}{3^2} = \frac{1}{9}\right)$		

2

    (a) $0.2 \times {}^-0.3 = 0.6$ is FALSE (⁻0.06) [page 39]

    (b) $\frac{4}{15} - \frac{7}{20} = \frac{25}{300}$ is TRUE but $-\frac{1}{12}$ is a simpler solution. [page 15]

    (c) $1\frac{3}{4} \div 4\frac{2}{3} = \frac{21}{56}$ is TRUE but $\frac{3}{8}$ is simpler. [pages 19, 38]

    (d) $65 < 21$ is FALSE (65 is greater than 21). [page 121]

3 [page 122]

17   35

4 (a) $10\ 000 = 10^4$ [page 23]

    (b) $0.001 = 10^{-3}$ [page 24]

5 (a) 256.87 = 2.5687 × 10² in standard form
        (scientific notation).   [page 25]

   (b) 0.0045 = 4.5 × 10⁻³ in standard form.   [page 25]

   (c) 1.155915 × 10°   [page 25]

6 (a) 31.567 = 32 to the nearest whole number.

   (b) 31.567 = 31.57 correct to 2 decimal places.

   (c) 31.567 = 30 correct to 1 significant figure.

7 $\frac{1}{9}$ = 0. (i.e., 0.1111 ... or 0.1 recurring).   [page 21]

8 $\frac{1}{4}$ = 0.25 which is a terminating decimal.   [page 21]

9 0.3 is a rational number because it can be obtained by
   dividing two integers (1/3).   [page 21]

10 √2 is an irrational number because it cannot be
    obtained by dividing two integers.   [page 21]

11 π is an irrational number (22/7 is only an
    approximation).   [page 21]

Number operations and algebra

12 With scientific calculators multiplication takes precedence
    over addition, so they give 2 + (3 × 4) = 14. Simple
    calculators perform operations in the order of input.   [page 32]

13 (a) 32 + 2 × 5 + 6 = 48 (multiplication before addition).

    (b) (32 + 2) × 5 + 6 = 176 (brackets first).

    (c) (32 + 2) × 5² + 6 = 856 (indices then brackets).

    (d) (20 + 7) (10 + 5) = 200 + 70 + 100 + 35 = 405.   [page 105]

    (e) $\frac{2.7 \times 1.08 \times 6.4}{1.27 \times 7.2 \times 2.4}$ = 0.9 (the key here is to 'cancel').

14 £14, £21, £35 $\left(\frac{2}{10}, \frac{3}{10} \text{ and } \frac{5}{10} \text{ of } £70\right)$ [page 62]

15 25% $\left(\frac{\text{difference}}{\text{original}} \times 100\% = \frac{75}{300} \times 100\%\right)$.   [page 41]

16 396 = 2 × 2 × 3 × 3 × 11.   [page 35]

17 $5a^3 b^2 + 5ab^3 = 5ab^2 (a^2 + b)$.   [page 106]

18 59° F (i.e, $\frac{9}{5} \times 15 + 32$).   [page 113]

19 All the expressions are equivalent to each other. [page 104]

20 (a) 9, 11, 13 are the next 3 numbers.   [page 101]

    (b) The nth term is $2n - 1$.   [page 101]

    (c) n^2 (The sum of the first 2 terms = 4 = 2^2;   [page 101]
         the sum of the first 3 terms = 9 = 3^2 ......).

Equations, functions and graphs

21 (a) $n = 1$.

   $(n + 2) = \sqrt{9}$, so $n = 3{-}2$. Note: by convention $\sqrt{9}$ indicates the positive root of 9. If you took it to mean both roots then you would have two answers: $n = 1$ and $n = {}^-5$.   [page 108]

   (b) 4 and $^-3$

   $(n + n^2 = 2n + 12$, so $n^2 - n - 12 = 0$.

   Therefore $(n - 4)(n + 3) = 0)$.   [page 108]

   (c) 2 and 3 $(a + b = 5, a \times b = 6)$.   [page 110]

   (d) $x = -\frac{1}{2}, y = 2$.   [page 110]

22.

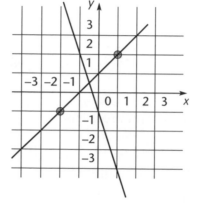

   (a) The y-intercept of the line is 1.

   (b) The gradient of the line is 1.

   (c) The equation of the line is $y = x + 1$.   [page 119]

23 (a) the y-intercept of $y = {}^-3x - 1$ is $^-1$.

   (b) The gradient of $y = {}^-3x - 1$ is $^-3$.

   (c) From the graph the point appears to be $\left(-\frac{1}{2}, \frac{1}{2}\right)$. Check whether this is so, by substituting in the equation of each line. At the point of intersection $y = {}^-3x - 1$ and $y = x + 1$. Therefore, $^-3x - 1 = x + 1$. Solve for x and substitute to find y. $\left(-\frac{1}{2}, \frac{1}{2}\right)$ is the point where the two lines intercept.   [page 119]

Mathematical reasoning and proof

24 (a) = of the same value   [page 174]

   (b) $\Rightarrow$ implies that   [page 175]

   (c) $\equiv$ is always true   [page 175]

(d) ∴ therefore it follows that [page 174]

(e) ≈ approximately equal to [page 23]

(f) ≥ greater than or equal to [page 121]

25 (a) Deductive proof: Let n be a number divided into k parts.

So, $n = 9k$

but $9 = 3 \times 3$

∴ $n = 3(3k)$, that is n is divisible by 3. [page 178]

(b) A trapezium has a pair of parallel sides but is not a parallelogram; so that statement is disproved by counter-example. [page 179]

(c) The 11 different scores are 2, 3, 4, 5, 6, 7, 8, 9, 10, 11, 12 as shown below:

	1	2	3	4	5	6
1	2	3	4	5	6	7
2	3	4	5	6	7	8
3	4	5	6	7	8	9
4	5	6	7	8	9	10
5	6	7	8	9	10	11
6	7	8	9	10	11	12

This is a proof by exhaustion. [page 182]

Measures

26 The SI prefix for 10^6 is 'mega' and the symbol M. [page 52]

27 (a) £3.41 to the nearest p (0.75×4.55).

(b) 4.40 gal (to 2 d.p.) (20 litres ≈ 20/4.55 gal) [page 56]

28 The relative error of $50° \pm 5°$ is ±10%. [page 49]

29 (a) The area of one face of a cube of side 2 cm is 4 cm^2.

(b) The volume of a cube of side 2 cm is 8 cm^3.

30 On a 1:25 000 map 50 mm represents 1.25 km on the ground.

Shape and space

31 A reflex angle is one which is greater than 180° but less than 360°. [pages 125–6]

32 The obtuse angles are 120°, the acute 60°.

33 (a) A regular hexagon has six lines of symmetry:

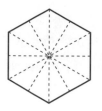

(b) A rectangle has two lines of symmetry:

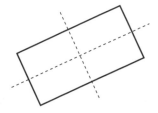

34 The shapes are all similar (equal angles and sides in proportion) but only A and C are congruent (same shape and same size), [page 138]

35 A square must be rotated 4 times through 90° in the same direction to return to its original position. [page 134]

36 Using Pythagoras' Theorem gives 13 cm ($\sqrt{(5^2 + 12^2)}$). [page 146]

37 (a) Both pairs of opposite sides are equal in length and parallel.

   (b) There are four equal angles which are right-angles.

   (c) Both diagonals are equal and bisect each other. [page 144]

38 The formula for the area of a trapezium is $\frac{1}{2}(a + b)h$. [page 150]

39 6 sq units ($\frac{1}{2} \times 3 \times 4$).

40 Draw the net of a 3, 4, 5 right-angled triangular prism 2 units long.

   (There are other possible nets.)

   (a) The volume of the opposite prism is 12 cu units (cross-section area × length).

   (b) The total surface area of the prism is 36 sq units.

   i.e., $(2 \times 6) + (2 \times 3) + (2 \times 4) + (2 \times 5)$.

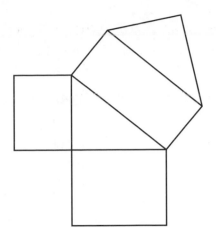

41 (a) The area of a sector of a third of a circle with radius
         3 cm is 9.42 sq units to 2 d.p. (i.e. $\frac{1}{3} \times \pi \times 3 \times 3$).   [page 153]

    (b) The length of the perimeter of the sector above is
         12.28 units (i.e., $3 + 3 + 2\pi \times \frac{3}{3}$).

42 An octahedron has 12 edges (Euler's relationship
    F + V = E + 2).   [page 156]

43 The faces of a regular dodecahedron are regular pentagons [page 155]

Probability and statistics

44 A bar chart is used for discrete data but a histogram is
    used for continuous data.   [pages 80–2]

45 The area of a pie chart represents the sample size –
    all the values of the sample together.   [pages 88–9]

46 Key features of a boxplot.

    LQ – lower quartile, UQ – upper quartile.   [page 87]

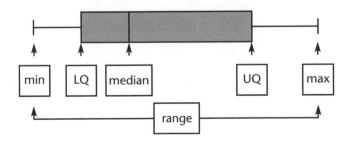

Height h	Class mid-point	Number	
$120 \leq h < 130$	125	9	1125
$130 \leq h < 140$	135	42	5670
$140 \leq h < 150$	145	69	10005
$150 \leq h < 160$	155	34	5270
$160 \leq h < 170$	165	6	990
Totals		160	23 060

(a) The median lies between 80 and 81 in rank order, so is in the 140–150 class.

(b) The mode is the class interval with the greatest number, so the mode is also 140–150.

(c) The mean = 23060/160 = 144.1 to 1 d.p.　　　　　[pages 83–6]

48　A tree diagram showing the possible outcomes of throwing a six-sided die and then tossing a coin (there are 12 possible outcomes)　　　　　[page 165]

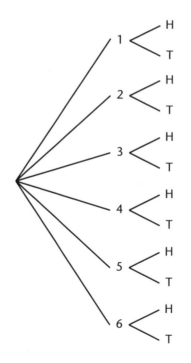

49 If two events are said to be 'independent' the chance of one occurring is unaffected by whether or not the other has occurred. For example, the events 'rolling a six' and 'tossing a head' are independent. Two events are said to be mutually exclusive if the occurrence of one excludes the possibility of the other occurring. For example, if a dice is rolled once, the events 'getting a 5' and 'getting an even score' are mutually exclusive.

[pages 164–7]

What now?

1. Think about those questions that you may have missed out of the audit. Has seeing the solutions reminded you about the topic? If so, a little revision may be enough. If not, perhaps the topic is not one you have studied before – most likely if you sat an intermediate rather than a higher GCSE paper.

2. What about questions where your answer was not right or not sufficiently complete? Was it a careless mistake or an underlying lack of understanding?

3. What about the questions you did get right? How convinced are you that you could answer any question on that topic? Were you relying on memory rather than understanding? Could you apply your skills, knowledge and understanding to more complex examples?

You should now make a list of topics that you need to:

▶ learn from scratch;

▶ re-learn;

▶ revise;

Audit question	Topic	Page(s)	Priority	When to do	Completed

> ▶ practice a bit more.

Revise and practise the topics you need to improve – how you order your priorities is up to you. To help keep up your morale, it might be sensible to alternate a topic which just needs 'brushing-up' with one that needs more work.

Once you are reasonably confident in all the topics, try the practice test in the next section. These questions require you to apply your skills, knowledge and understanding.

Practice assessment test

Purpose

Sometime during your training course you may need to provide evidence that your mathematics subject knowledge and understanding are to the required standard. You will probably have to do this by satisfactorily completing a test under examination conditions. The following test includes examples of the types of question you might be expected to answer. Use it both for examination practice and to familiarise yourself with questions which require you to apply your knowledge and understanding.

Part A comprises examples of calculations and statements that are not correct in some way. You need to correct or complete the answer, and say what misconception caused the error. Part B has examples of longer questions involving several topics.

Set aside at least an hour to work through all the questions. If you have any problems, leave those questions and come back to them at the end. Only look at the solutions once you have done as much as possible on the whole test.

Part A

Correct or amend the following:

1 'Multiplication makes bigger.'

2 'Subtraction makes smaller.'

3 '$0.3 \times {}^-0.3 = 0.9$.'

4 '$52.3 \times 10 = 52.30$.'

5 '$\pi = 22/7$.'

6 '$123456789 = 12.3 \times 10^7$ in standard form correct to 3 significant figures.'

7 '$3^{-2} = {}^-9$.'

8 '$\frac{1}{4} + \frac{2}{5} = \frac{3}{9}$'

9   'The following are equivalent to $\frac{1}{5}$:

(a) $\frac{3}{15}$:   (b) 25%;   (c) two tenths;   (d) 0.5.'

10 'To find the original cost of an item reduced by 15% to £850: £850 × 15/100 = £127.50. £850 + £127.50 = £977.50.'

11 'Congruent triangles are not similar.'

12 'A right-angled triangle with sides of 3 and 4 must have the third side length 5.'

13 'Scaling a shape by a factor of 2 doubles the perimeter and area.'

14 'Discrete data must be whole numbers.'

15 'If I throw a fair six-sided dice 60 times I will get 10 ones.'

Part B

16 The following data shows the result of an experiment to test reaction times of a group of people before and after some training. Represent this data graphically in a way that enables you to compare the two sets of results.

Person	Before	After
A	34	28
B	37	29
C	39	29
D	41	30
E	41	31
F	43	33
G	45	35
H	54	36
I	67	39
J	78	41

What is the average reaction time before training? after training?

(Use both median and mean and explain why mode does not apply here.)

Compare the ranges. How would you explain the differences you have found?

17 Look at the following pattern:

3 + 1 = 4

5 + 3 + 1 = 9

$7 + 5 + 3 + 1 = 16$

What is the next line?

What is the nth line?

18 There are two numbers a and b. When you add them together you get 25. When you subtract one from the other you get 11. What are a and b?

19 Calculate the point of intersection of the graphs of the equations $y = x + 4$ and $y = {}^-2x + 5$. Which is the steeper of these two graphs? Explain your reasoning.

20 On a square grid mark points A (2, 1) and B (1, 2). Rotate each point 90° anti-clockwise around the origin, resulting in points C and D respectively.

(a) Name the resulting shape ABCD. Calculate the area and perimeter of the shape ABCD.

(b) How many lines of symmetry does it have?

(c) Imagine that this shape is the cross-section of a solid metal bar of length 5 units. What volume of metal is there in the bar?

(d) How many planes of symmetry does the bar have?

21 Imagine you are playing a game for 2 players which involves tossing a dice and a coin. You win if you get a six or a head. Otherwise your partner wins.

(a) Show the possible outcomes on a tree diagram.

(b) Is the game fair?

(c) Are the events 'tossing a head' and 'winning' mutually exclusive?

22 Prove or disprove the following:

(a) If a shape is a kite and it also has sides of equal length then it must be a square.

(b) If a number is divisible by 12 then it is divisible by 3.

Solutions to practice test

As you check your solutions make some notes for yourself to indicate whether your solution was:

(a) correct and complete;

(b) correct but missing some detail, for example, units or number of decimal places;

(c) incorrect due to a careless error;

(d) incorrect due to some misunderstanding;

(e) missing.

Part A

For convenience, the question is repeated.

1 'Multiplication makes bigger.'

   Not always, multiplication by a fraction makes smaller.

2 'Subtraction makes smaller.'

   Not always, subtraction of a negative number makes larger.

3 '$0.3 \times {}^-0.3 = 0.9$'.

   Needs correcting to $0.3 \times {}^-0.3 = {}^-0.09$

4 '$52.3 \times 10 = 52.30$.'

   Needs correcting to 523.0

5 '$\pi = 22/7$.'

   No, this is an approximation. π is an irrational number so cannot be written exactly as a fraction.

6 '$123456789 = 12.3 \times 10^7$ in standard form correct to 3 significant figures.'

   Should be 1.23×10^8 correct to 3 significant figures (in standard form the number must be between 1 and 10).

7 '$3^{-2} = {}^-9$'.

   $3^{-2} = \left(\frac{1}{3}\right)^2 = \frac{1}{9} = $ (i.e., $0.1111 \dots$).

8 '$\frac{1}{4} + \frac{2}{5} = \frac{3}{9}$.'

   $\frac{1}{4} + \frac{2}{5} = \frac{5}{20} + \frac{8}{20} = \frac{13}{20}$

9 'The following are equivalent to $\frac{1}{5}$:

   (a) $\frac{3}{15}$; (b) 25%; (c) two tenths; (d) 0.5.'

   (a) $\frac{3}{15} = \frac{1}{5}$: (b) $25\% = \frac{25}{100} = \frac{1}{4}$: (c) $\frac{2}{10} = \frac{1}{5}$; (d) $0.5 = \frac{5}{10} = \frac{1}{2}$;

10 'To find the original cost of an item reduced by 15% to £850.'
    £850 × 15/100 = £127.50. £850 + £127.50 = £977.50

    85% of original price   = £850

    original price   = £850 × 100/85

    original price   = £1000

11 'Congruent triangles are not similar.'

    Yes they are. ('Similar' shapes have the same shape but may differ in size. Congruent triangles are identical in size and shape; they are a special kind of similar triangles) – but similar triangles are not necessarily congruent.

12 'A right-angled triangle with sides of 3 and 4 must have the third side length 5.'

    No, only if the side of length 4 is NOT the hypotenuse.

13 'Scaling a shape by a factor of 2 doubles the perimeter and area.'

The perimeter doubles but the area quadruples.

14 'Discrete data must be whole numbers.'

No, discrete data are in categories so can be names or numbers (e.g. colours or shoe sizes).

15 'If I throw a fair six-sided dice 60 times I will get 10 ones.'

Unlikely. The actual number could be anything between 0 and 60; 10 would be the average over a very large number of throws.

Part B

16 The following data shows the result of an experiment to test reaction times of a group of people before and after some training. Represent this data graphically in a way that enables you to compare the two sets of results.

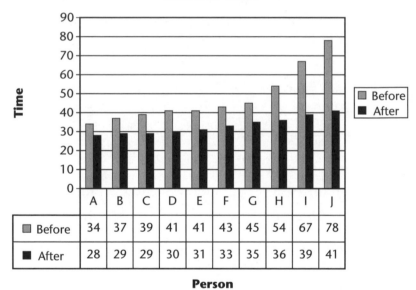

Reaction Times

Person	A	B	C	D	E	F	G	H	I	J
Before	34	37	39	41	41	43	45	54	67	78
After	28	29	29	30	31	33	35	36	39	41

Note: The data does not have to be shown on the compound bar chart as above. Also note the convention of gaps between bar chart columns for discrete data (in this case each person is a 'discrete' category).

What is the average reaction time before training? after training?

(Use both median and mean and explain why mode does not apply here.)

	Before training	After training
Mean	47.9 (to 1 d. p.)	33.1 (to 1 d. p.)
Median	42	32
Range	44	13

Mode is not an appropriate summary measure. This data is a comparison of individual changes in reaction time – each result is only recorded once so the most frequent time is meaningless.

Compare the ranges. How would you explain the differences you have found?

Training reduces reaction time. It has greatest effect on those with the slowest initial reaction times, i.e., the least 'fit'.

17 Look at the following pattern:

$3 + 1 = 4$

$5 + 3 + 1 = 9$

$7 + 5 + 3 + 1 = 16$

What is the next line?

$9 + 7 + 5 + 3 + 1 = 25$

What is the nth line?

$(2n + 1) + (2n - 1) + \ldots 5 + 3 + 1 = (n + 1)^2$

18 There are two numbers a and b. When you add them together you get 25. When you subtract one from the other you get 11. What are a and b?

$a + b = 25$

$a - b = 11$

adding

$2a = 36$

so $a = 18$

substituting 18 for a

$18 + b = 25$

so $b = 7$

19 Calculate the point of intersection of the graphs of the equations $y = x + 4$ and $y = {}^{-}2x + 5$.

At the point of intersection:

$x + 4 = {}^{-}2x + 5$

$3x + 4 = 5$

$3x = 1$

$x = \frac{1}{3}$

$y = \frac{1}{3} + 4$

$y = 4\frac{1}{3}$

Which is the steeper of these two graphs? Explain your reasoning.

$y = {}^-2x + 5$. In the general expression for a straight line

$y = mx + c$, m is the gradient. Although $^-2$ is a negative gradient the line is steeper than $y = x + 4$ which has a gradient of 1.

20 On a square grid mark points A (2, 1) and B (1, 2). Rotate each point 90° anti-clockwise around the origin, resulting in points C and D.

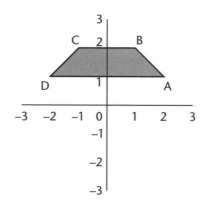

(a) Name the resulting shape ABCD:

Trapezium.

Calculate the area and perimeter of the shape ABCD:

Area = 1 × (2 + 4)/2 = 3 sq units

(half the sum of parallel sides × height).

Perimeter = AB + BC + CD + DA

$AB^2 = 1^2 + 1^2 = 2$ (Pythagoras) so AB = $\sqrt{2}$, CD also = $\sqrt{2}$

Perimeter = $\sqrt{2} + 2 + \sqrt{2} + 4$ units = 8.83 units

(correct to 2 decimal places).

(b) How many lines of symmetry does it have?

One (from mid-point BC to mid-point AD).

(c) Imagine that this shape is the cross-section of a solid metal bar of length 5 units. What volume of metal is there in the bar?

15 cu units (Area of cross-section × length).

(d) How many planes of symmetry does the bar have?

Two.

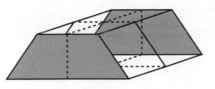

21 Imagine you are playing a game for 2 players which involves tossing a dice and a coin. You win if you get a six or a head. Otherwise your partner wins.

(a) Show the possible outcomes on a tree diagram.

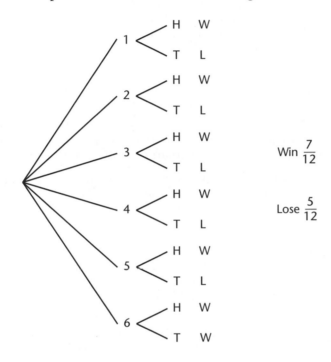

(b) Is the game fair?

No, since it is possible for your partner to win in more than half of the possibilities.

(c) Are the events 'tossing a head' and 'winning' mutually exclusive?

No – it is possible to do both.

22 Prove or disprove the following:

(a) If a shape is a kite and it also has sides of equal length then it must be a square.

Disproved by counter-example: a rhombus has sides of equal length but is not a square.

(b) If a number is divisible by 12 then it is divisible by 3.

Deductive proof:

Let n be any number divisible by 12.

Then $n = 12k$ where k is a whole number

But $12k = 3 \times 4k$ which is divisible by 3 so n is divisible by 3.

Now what?

How did you get on with the practice test? How long did it take to complete?

Knowing particular mathematical facts and techniques is not the same as being able to apply these in differing contexts. You may have found that your understanding is not yet sufficiently secure.

Work through the solutions to any question with which you had major problems. Note which topics were problematic, and work through the relevant section of the book (the index or contents will help you to find the right sections). Once you have done that try the question again. If you are still having problems you may need to acquire a GCSE higher-level textbook to get additional help and practice questions.

You should have been able to complete the test in 1 to $1\frac{1}{2}$ hours – if it took much longer you need to think about why that might have been. It may be some time since you did a mathematics examination and you need to gain more practice.

Once you have checked up on all areas of the mathematical knowledge needed to meet the ITT requirements, think carefully about whether you are ready to provide evidence of your understanding. A good strategy for doing this is to go back through the audit and practice questions to see if you think you could answer different questions like the ones shown; then try to construct testing questions for yourself of the same sort of type. If you are in contact with a colleague, try exchanging questions.

Acknowledgements

Thank you to the Open University PGCE students who used and provided feedback on the audit and practice questions.

Developing a mathematical dictionary

The index gives page references to many of the mathematical terms used in this book. However, neither the selection of words nor the detail given is likely to be a perfect match for your own needs. Consequently, you are urged to start creating your own mathematical dictionary. This will give entries that are useful to you personally and, in addition, you will benefit from expressing the ideas in your own words.

It is suggested that you use sheets of A4 writing paper or a notebook to make entries to your dictionary. As you work through the book pick out any words or phrases which are themselves unfamiliar or which are being used in an unfamiliar way. Write them down then make notes (which might include diagrams) about what you understand by them and add clear page references to remind you where they appear in the book. Leave some space after each entry in case you wish to add further information later as your understanding of a particular idea grows.

You may also wish to reserve a section of your dictionary for mathematical symbols and notation.

Alternatively you may wish to create your dictionary electronically using a word-processing package. That way you can rearrange your entries at any stage and only print them out when you are ready.

Index